WHEN THE WHIPPOORWILL SANG

WHEN THE WHIPPOORWILL SANG

A Memoir of Rural Life During the
Twilight of the Segregated South

Arthur Lee Ford, Jr.

Center for Louisiana Studies
University of Louisiana at Lafayette
2008

Center for Louisiana Studies
University of Louisiana at Lafayette
© 2008 by Center for Louisiana Studies
P.O. Box 40831
Lafayette, LA 70504-0831

http://cls.louisiana.edu

Library of Congress Cataloging-in-Publication Data

Ford, Arthur Lee.
When the whippoorwill sang : a memoir of rural life during the twilight of the segregated South / Arthur Lee Ford, Jr.
p. cm.
ISBN 1-887366-84-9 (alk. paper)
1. Ford, Arthur Lee. 2. African Americans--Louisiana--Bossier Parish--Biography. 3. African Americans--Louisiana--Bossier Parish--Social conditions--20th century. 4. African Americans--Segregation--Louisiana--Bossier Parish--History--20th century. 5. Bossier Parish (La.)--Social conditions--20th century. 6. Bossier Parish (La.)--Rural conditions--20th century. 7. Bossier Parish (La.)--Biography. 8. Cotton trade--Louisiana--Bossier Parish--History--20th century. I. Title.

F377.B6F67 2008
305.896'073076397092--dc22
[B]

2008023740

CONTENTS

FOREWORD
by James D. Wilson Jr. vii

ACKNOWLEDGEMENTS ix

INTRODUCTION xiii

CHAPTER ONE
The Lake Bottoms: Wardview 1

CHAPTER TWO
Sharecropping on the Lake Bottoms......................... 41

CHAPTER THREE
Champions of Wardview... 59

CHAPTER FOUR
Early Family Heritage.. 77

CHAPTER FIVE
Early School Days 93

CHAPTER SIX
Family Years in Bolinger 109

CHAPTER SEVEN
High School Independence 155

CHAPTER EIGHT
Back Home in Bolinger.. 175

EPILOGUE 189

APPENDIX
Southern Rural Negro Dialect 197

FOREWORD

When the Whippoorwill Sang is a unique memoir. Arthur Lee Ford, Jr. makes the common, everyday – perhaps even mundane – aspects of southern rural life, regardless of race, interesting and exciting. Unlike many of the memoirs set during the era of segregation, which usually cover unique events and exceptional stories of racial conflict, Ford's story focuses on the subtle constraints imposed on all rural African Americans in the segregated South and the central dilemma that defined their lives – a bounded existence imposed on an otherwise happy individual with boundless aspirations and abilities.

Like many African Americans who came of age in the segregated South, once Ford was old enough he fled in search of the opportunity and freedom that most Americans took for granted, first to California then to western Michigan. This soon presented Ford with another internal conflict, one that is probably more widespread among African Americans than most realize: the urgency of fleeing the constraints of the South juxtaposed against the later onset of the notion that those were somehow the best days of their life and a desire to return to that simpler lifestyle. This phenomenon is clearly evidenced by the widespread practice of sending African American children southward to find their roots and even in the large number of northern-born students that are drawn to the historically black colleges and universities of the South.

Without a doubt the most striking aspect of Ford's memoir is the author's ability to demonstrate with amazing clarity the striking similarities in the lives of African American cotton pickers and their southern white counterparts, at least in the waning years of segregation. Family, work, community, all were central concerns of everyday life much more so than racial matters. While burning crosses and nooses hanging from trees might more graphically convey the racism of the segregated South, it is the much more commonplace internal turmoil and emotional damage inflicted upon both black and white southerners during that era that is hardest to grasp and the most difficult to erase.

When the Whippoorwill Sang makes it crystal clear that no episode in American history is as rigidly defined by racial lines as generally thought and even more importantly that black and white southerners probably have much more in common that anyone is comfortable admitting.

James D. Wilson, Jr.

ACKNOWLEDGEMENTS

First I would like to thank Mr. Odie Lee Gore, Jr. and his sister Miss Glenda Gore for sharing so many facts, photographs and memories of their family and Plantation (farm to them) and of the Lake Bottoms. They played a major role in making this book possible.

Mr. John Little, a son of Mrs. Hester and Mr. Willie Little has proven to be a walking encyclopedia on the people and earlier times of the Lake Bottoms. He verified, clarified and presented facts about the Little family saga on the Lake Bottoms and indeed played another major role in making this book possible.

I want to thank all my family and friends who encouraged me some fierce to get this book done so the people will know. My two sons Frederick and Douglas kept bailing me out on the computer as I constantly worked myself into a corner. My daughter, Natalie, was always getting my attention and slapping my wrists about some literary corrections.

Thanks to Mr. and Mrs. Margaret and Edward Haskin, Jr. who welcomed me with understanding of the project on which I was working. Margaret is the daughter of Raymond T. (Bim) Little and talked about the good deeds of her hard working father. She and Eddy took me to Hester's Chapel and showed me all the wonderful improvements made to the church since I was there in about 1963. I was the guitar player for the Hearts of Harmony at that time and was so busy enjoying the clapping of hands and tapping of feet inside that church I never noticed that there were improvements needing to be made. They always welcomed me as though I was one of their own.

I would finally like to thank all the people who will go

unnamed that I met in my travels in many different states of our country discussing facts about many of the events and happenings covered in this book and promised them that they would get copies. You know who you are! My many thanks to the helpful people of the Bossier Parish Historical Society for spurring me on as well as those of the Center for Louisiana Studies at the University of Louisiana at Lafayette.

A Note On Language

There are a great number of reasons I wrote about an original American experience. Language is just one reason. Words and phrases used in the past to communicate with and refer to people and things would be just short of a crime in today's world. During the days of racial segregation the words Negro, colored, boy, gal, aiy (Aunt), Unca (Uncle), niggra, nigger, and other references to African-Americans were the norm, and not just in the South. There is almost infinite film footage and other sound recordings of the 20th Century to prove it. Some of the words and terms I used in this book were not only the same ones used at that time but were meant to place the reader in that setting for the sake of understanding, even when in reality the words in those days were much more brash. Back then "Black" and "African-American" had not yet reached or penetrated the American psyche, let alone begun to indicate something positive.

Even in those days African-American people were terribly offended by the derogatory use, and the references meant by the use, of these words and terms. What hurt more was the fact that practitioners paid feelings no regard, for they felt it was their natural right and privilege to call a Negro whatever they wanted to. The intention of the users was to humiliate, not only because they could but because it made them feel superior. When I heard someone use the adjective "black" in those days it humiliated a person worse than the word nigger. The most denigrating putdown to a Negro was to be called a "black nigger."

The terms Negroid, Caucasoid, and Mongoloid are scientific-social ones describing what we have been taught are the three basic races of peoples inhabiting planet earth. If you study other languages you will see that the word negro means the color black. History has shown us that people can take anything and interpret it to mean whatever they want it to mean. If they theorize something to mean a certain "thing" they will not hesitate to peddle it as the truth. This is the point where I believe it behooves everyone to be discerning.

Arthur Lee Ford, Jr.

INTRODUCTION

I know there are hundreds of books about the subjects on which I am going to write that remain unwritten. They exist in the minds of people who experienced awesome racism, racial segregation and Jim Crow laws supported by intense terrorist Klan activity in their cruelest incarnations since the Emancipation Proclamation as well as the Thirteenth and Fourteenth Amendments to the constitution of the United States, and still managed to survive. It would be of phenomenal human interest if somehow those very stories could be told. To some that experience is a nightmare to be forgotten, to others it is true American history not to be forgotten. I count myself among the latter because of the affect our past has had on the destinies of us all. Even though I have mentioned only the two extremes, there are people living today whose lives run the gamut of that original American experience, especially in their inheritance from the preceding generations, which was not by choice.

Finding my place in the flow of American society has always been a challenge, and I long ago realized that it is because of the way I have been forced to think, a result of having to constantly deal with the backlash of the actions and beliefs of others. So I had to become a counter puncher and a trail blazer of survival. After many knocks and bruises it didn't take me long to figure out that insistence on existence in itself was, and still is, a challenge to the system under which I live. Long before I finished high school I have always asked myself, "How is simple intelligence a challenge to a system?" This alone tells me a whole story about the system and I now no longer wonder how. I have always believed that what one thinks is what one does. So I have gotten the message, "You are a member of our society who is not suppose to know how to think," many times more than I cared to. I know all too well how Dred Scott, Frederick Douglass, Nat Turner, Susan B. Anthony and John Brown felt. Growing up in the South during racial segregation and Jim Crow I learned that my experiences were more in tune with slavery than with the vast, dog-eat-dog, immigrant-influenced way of life we experience in America today. Actually America has never been without immigrants; besides, who today among immigrants is going to stand on American soil and yell out loud to the world that they are not American? I am not saying whether immigration is bad or good for the United States; I am saying I can't go back and live in the past, slavery, but that I was unprepared for the future, in which I now live. However, speaking from experience I do believe that once we all as Americans direct our actions toward productivity, for whatever reason, we can't go wrong. People helping people is what the world is about and we have a long way to go before ethnic distinction is eliminated, as long as one believes that.

In other words the United States, in theory, is the land of the free and maybe it will actually reach that status one day. In reality, today, it is the land of polarization, which could very well explain serious infighting and seemingly opposing or irreconcilable social factions. Polarization is a sure indicator of the presence of the restraint of someone or some class, ethnic group, or race of people. However, people that polarize by choice believe in freedom only for themselves, and at the same time are audacious enough to consider themselves as main stream as anyone. As a result some people are denied assimilation while certain other inhabitants take valuable resources from society but refuse to assimilate. No free society is intolerant of its inhabitants. Moreover, no society is free that doesn't show it. People that are denied assimilation in our country must always be creative to survive and live here.

And every time they create something it gets "borrowed" or "taken" or "claimed" by members of so-called mainstream society as their own. This leaves the rejected group "in the cold" and "disregarded." So the rejected group or groups remain in the position of incessantly "feeding" a country that suppresses them. Therefore, society's rejected people are in constant threat of displacement because of deliberate exploitation. In reality, as human history reveals, free thinking people mobilize with purpose, show respect for others, and try to help the less fortunate, even though it may cost them dearly in many ways. Polarization demonstrates the exact opposite. When individuals exhibit freedom of mind and body, the group as a whole will generate a totally different energy from what exists in our society and world today, especially as some of us continue struggling to move forward.

A truly amalgamated big picture is something that can't be faked. African Americans, mostly descendants of slaves, and Native Americans talk among themselves to this day with great concern about their disenfranchisement, and how the benefits of that disenfranchisement are enjoyed by a constant flow of incoming immigrants, along with the omnipresent descendants of the oppressors themselves. The continued discussion among African-Americans concerns how it is an abomination to have been forced to work themselves up from slavery in a highly competitive society, merely to compete.

It is not difficult at all to see clearly what the intention of segregationists was, and, for that matter, still is. The evidence is scattered throughout the landscape. The thought patterns of segregationist politicians, schoolmasters, plantation and business owners are clearly defined by tangible evidence, which cannot be denied. Those of us endowed with vision and wisdom owe it to all the innocent victims of slavery and Jim Crow to provide at least an explanation as to what happened and how it happened. This also includes the innocent people within the oppressor groups. In my opinion, everyone deserves at least a chance to possess a clear and open mind. But it is evident that the segregationists did not, and do not now, think that way. Segregationists think that the shortest route to their success and survival is to divide and conquer, and conquer and divide, and, in the process, destroy people that are physically or ideologically different from them. And when an individual doesn't think or do things like a segregationist, it is likely that the segregationist will wage war against the individual, even without the individual knowing it. Individuals with open minds do not entertain thoughts of oppressing or suppressing other minds or bodies.

Twentieth-century Southern Negroes required a unique mindset to survive, like Negroes in any other century. It left little or no time for humor because a constant struggle for survival continued from slavery and without interruption. Now if you find humor in that you're good. But at the same time, we played music and sports as hard as we worked, attempting to find relief from the constant grind. I was a pursuer of academics but with a real-world twist, an endeavor void of fantasy. I lived in the world of reality, replete with raw human emotion, pain, hunger, hate and love. The worlds of academics and music always gave me a sense of relief, that healing feeling, real therapy, living without stepping on the toes of others.

I hail from the cotton fields of Louisiana, in the northwest corner of the state. From the banks of the Old River near which the famous Red River flows, near a place called Wardview, to the Hills of Bossier Parish in a little settlement called Bolinger, and on to Plain Dealing.

The Wardview settlement was a huge flatland farm area where many plantations operated, cultivating mainly cotton. It stretched from a few miles northwest of St. Mary, a little settle-

ment west of Plain Dealing along Highway 2, all the way north
to a place called Half Moon, and onward to the Arkansas-
Louisiana state line. From the years long before the 1940s and
on through the 1960s, Wardview was buzzing, really humming
with human activity. Negro people lived in old houses on the
plantations and sharecropped. Other Negro people were transported, or trucked, to the Wardview area from surrounding areas to help work the cotton fields. When I came to understand
the structure of things, it was plain to see that the people in
surrounding areas were already all too familiar with Wardview
because Wardview had served as a proving ground for them
also. Both the people in the surrounding areas and the people
in Wardview referred to the Wardview area as "The Lake Bottoms," or "The Lake," or "The Bottoms."

Bolinger was located seven miles south of the Lou-
isiana-Arkansas state line on Highway 3 and the largest portion of three miles north of Plain Dealing. In those days
Plain Dealing and Bolinger also hummed with human activity.
Bolinger had pumping oil wells, a sawmill, juke joints, stores,
and churches. There were many thriving residents, colored and
white. Bolinger even had a little one-room school house, at one
point in time, called Glover Hill School, for colored people.
Among several other important businesses, Plain Dealing actually had a cotton Brokerage where huge bales of cotton were
docked and shipped out by rail. In my early youth there was a
racially segregated movie theater in Plain Dealing, only it wasn't
known as such in those days. It was called the "picture show"
by the people, but officially known as the "Fox Theatre." Colored patrons watched from an upstairs balcony and the white
patrons watched from the main floor seats. Daddy took me to
the picture show once when I was a little one but all I remember seeing was part of the opening cartoon. I never went to the
Fox Theatre again and do not know when it closed.

Plain Dealing mainly consisted of residential communities referred to as "hills," such as the DeMoss Hill, the Crawford Hill and the Gustafson Hill. Crawford Hill in the 1930s and 1940s was located in what eventually became the white folks' section of Plain Dealing, just north of downtown, but at that time it housed a number of Negro residents. Some of the Negro students of early Carrie Martin High School had to walk past the white folks' school, Plain Dealing High, to get to their school. Some of my sisters experienced that and they also heard some interesting morning songs of recitation coming from the windows of the Plain Dealing High School buildings as they walked past them. Crawford Hill also provided Negro maids and other help to white households, as a matter of convenience. Then, from the mid-1940s onward Crawford Hill started becoming less Negro. The "Negro exodus" continued until that part of town became all white. As a result, the Negroes living in Plain Dealing became primarily south-side and southwest-side dwellers.

The Gustafson Hill, otherwise known by the Negroes in those days as "Starvation Hill," set on the south side just slightly southwest of Carrie Martin High School, across the railroad tracks that ran next to the school; the DeMoss Hill set on Plain Dealing's southwest side. Although these two Hills were clearly defined in terms of location, racially segregated, and completely inhabited by Negroes, there were concentrations of Negro inhabitants north, east, south, and west of them, stretching from downtown Plain Dealing to span the entire territory. Yet, some rival social groups existed between the two Hills. The Gustafson and DeMoss Hills at some point came to host their own quaint little honky-tonks and stores.

Most of the white folks in Plain Dealing made it very clear in many ways that they didn't want Negroes living near them. For instance, a cross was burned on the yard of our school bus driver, who lived a short distance east, actually on the eastern edge of where old Crawford Hill once existed. I remember riding the bus the next day and listening to the kids talk about it. I heard the driver say in very firm and deliberate words as he looked in his overhead rearview mirror at us, "Hush! Watch your mouths!" The driver never relocated his family, and I never since heard anything else about it. I just don't think that the Mayor and many other people in Plain Dealing knew how many of our bus drivers and teachers worked in intelligent and subtle ways to help maintain racial peace in Plain Dealing. I can remember when Mr. Olga (R.J.) Player, a prominent Plain Dealing Negro resident and absolutely devoted family man, made his living driving a school bus and hauling pulpwood. Mr. Player spearheaded a gallant effort in those days of racial segregation, attempting to organize Negro citizens and others to promote positive endeavors of community cohesion among all the people. At that time, I can also remember how some of the Negro Baptist Churches in Plain Dealing actively promoted open dialogue among themselves.

My own true story is that of a Negro boy growing up in the racially segregated South, trying to find his way in a world of oblivion; one in which what you thought and felt as a Negro person meant nothing and was of absolutely no consequence as far as the status quo was concerned; a place where, as a Negro, you were more likely destined to develop your own individual "feel" for survival.

But little did they know, I loved being left alone, for I was bred and born in the Brier Patch. When you live in the Brier Patch, they don't suspect that you have a mind and think you don't know anything. Of course, the "Brier Patch" is a figure of speech used by slaves and passed through the generations of the descendants of slaves; it described a life-or-death struggle. It was a part of the universal language of oppression.

When the term "Brier Patch" was mentioned, everybody knew you had nowhere to go, but up. The Brier Patch is where you learn to play the hand that nature dealt you. You learn through trial and error, nip and tuck, because all you have is yourself. You must keep your mistakes to a minimum because there is no safety net beneath you. The Brier Patch is where you develop strong trust in your mind and body. You become a great improviser of your methods of survival, for conventionality does not work for you. These are just some of the conditions under which you become undoubtedly self-made.

I will present this book in chapters, attempting to maintain the integrity of order and chronology. I will tell you in a manner describing and depicting events, experiences and memories in the early years of my youth from six months of age to about ten years of age, along with a brief accounting of my true family heritage. Then it will be up to you to hold on, because I am going to take you on a rough-and-tumble ride on the bucking horse of racial segregation and Jim Crow as I tell you about the later years of my youth. There will be no cut-and-dried pattern as I move from early years to later years because life itself didn't work that way. Periodically, while discussing the happenings of my early years I will make quick references to episodes and events of the later years, and vice versa. By the time I was eighteen years of age, when I left the South, I already realized that I had experienced a way of life that only some Americans knew still existed, and one that most Americans put forth every effort to deny. I can't let them get away with that because denying my heritage is denying me and denying our true American history. The day I left Louisiana in late May of 1965 Bossier Parish was as racially segregated as it was in 1925. Nevertheless, please accompany me to a time and place where racial segregation ruled, and where cotton was king.

CHAPTER ONE

The Lake Bottoms: Wardview

Of all the lessons in United States and world history that Mr. Wright taught us in school, the one fact I never forgot was that all the states within the United States have counties, except for Louisiana. Louisiana has parishes. I always wondered why but never got around to asking Mr. Wright. If that isn't interesting, I don't know what is. Mr. Wright, "Fess" as we called him, or "Fessa Wright," as the old folks called him, would walk, pacing the floor, while discussing subject matter. He would ask the class a question while walking past you and quickly spin around, thrusting his arm straight outward and pointing at you, knowing you weren't listening. I think Fess caused a lot of heart attacks; we just didn't die.

By now, I would think most of us have heard of the Louisiana Purchase. I figured if this vast piece of land was purchased by the United States government from the French, it would be only fitting that some French influence be shown therein. So, if you know anything about the Louisiana Purchase you know that the State of Louisiana is what's left of it, at least for our purpose here, even though the entire territory is now several states within the United States of America. Having said that, Louisiana, in my opinion, remains more representative of French influence than any other state in the Union. Yet, with a more detailed focus on Louisiana, you will notice that the names attributed to many of its parishes originate from the last names of Frenchmen. Bossier Parish, then, is no exception. Of course, this is not to say that the French necessarily established or caused slavery in Bossier Parish, although some of the French brought slaves to Louisiana long before the fact.

Yet, one can clearly see that slavery did not necessarily come with the territory. Slavery came because of the territory, the land, the soil, the richness of which was and still is highly productive. And as the centuries have shown, it most definitely served its purpose.

At a time when the world economy showed great demand for textiles, the textile industry responded with a great demand for the production of cotton. As a result, cotton plantations sprang up like pine trees in a forest at the hands of businessmen seeking economic wealth. Caucasian businessmen who could afford it, as well as some of those who couldn't afford it, lapped up the opportunities like a big plate of hot-buttered pancakes floating in syrup, and, in the process, obtained thousands of acres of rich land and accessed free slave labor to boot. The plantation way of life took hold and stuck to Louisiana like a magnet to steel, determining the destinies of real human lives and consuming them from birth to death. This tradition was passed from generation to generation of Louisianans and remains to this day well represented and documented in Bossier Parish. Northwest Bossier Parish, in and around Wardview, the Lake Bottoms, supported several cotton plantations during the days of segregation, when I grew up in Bossier Parish, and the economy of that area thrived because of it.

When sunup came to the Lake Bottoms it brought with it an awakening of predetermined, deliberate plantation activity. Although, activity inside the houses stirred long before the sun rose. Households would be already teeming with the efforts of large families preparing for daybreak, for sunup and sundown were the age-old time-tested signals by which plantation life progressed. People would arise long before daybreak, doing things like readying the children for work in the cotton fields, cooking and preparing food for breakfast, and most importantly "fixing," or packing their "dinner bucket." In those days, lunch in the cotton fields was always referred to as "dinner." Also, people in the hills and other surrounding areas were up before daybreak doing the same things because they had to "catch the cotton truck" to go work the cotton fields for a living. Catching the cotton truck meant having to get out of bed even earlier because they had to allow for travel time to the cotton fields of the Lake Bottoms. In the Hills and other areas surrounding the Lake Bottoms in Bossier Parish, this would be 3:00 a.m. or sooner. This was just one reason among many that people went to bed early in the evening.

The term "cotton truck" referred to any vehicle used to transport workers to and from the cotton fields. Vehicle owners installed benches that ran along the walls of the truck bed, even the portion behind the cab. The procedure resembled that employed by the old late nineteenth and early twentieth century-styled prison wagons that transported prisoners. The cotton trucks' beds would usually be covered with removable heavy-duty tarps. In that area I always would hear Negro people refer to the coverings as "topoleyon," never "tarpaulin" or "tarp." I can remember riding inside the trucks during cotton production seasons for years. People riding in the trucks were very interesting to observe. I loved seeing the spirits of sad-looking folks stimulated and actually lifted at times through communication. There was seldom much conversation among the riders as a vehicle advanced toward the cotton fields; however, that changed a bit as the season progressed, allowing the people to get to know one another better. Some riders would still be sleepy and would close their eyes as they rode the trucks. Riders in each vehicle mostly showed respect toward each other and usually bonded as a temporary group. I would observe everyone noticing everyone else, just looking and thinking. I would look at different people and often wonder what their individual lives were like. And I always wondered if those people were determined to improve their position in life, as I was. One thing I knew for sure, riding the cotton trucks provided lots of time to think and reflect, as long as you freed up your mind to do so.

In those days, the premium was on having or being part of a big family. The more working members there were in a family, the more revenue the family generated. In plantation terminology, each working person was called a "head" or a "hand." So the plan of mothers and fathers, and of the plantation owners, was to provide as many heads, or hands, as possible. And when cotton was ready for picking, of course, even the little ones were included, because the money was dependent upon quantity. Chopping cotton, on the other hand, required experience, strength, and endurance, for the workday was long and hard on the body and mind, and the pay was thirty cents per hour. So the little ones didn't normally participate in chopping. The sharecroppers, or people who lived "on the place," had no say in what they did for the plantation owners, and when it came to work priorities they were given to the sharecroppers over the hill people, or people who were trucked in. Of course, these "priorities" were always meant to favor the plantation. After all, the sharecroppers were the ones who lived on the plantation and were constantly working anyway. The system worked against workers who were trucked in, for they were paid only for their actual work on the plantation. For instance, if it rained there wouldn't be any work for hired help. For the trucked-in workers the rain affected both chopping and picking because both took place outside, in the elements. The sharecroppers were not affected by the rain much because there was always a variety of plantation chores needing to be done, many of which could be done inside, sheltering them from the elements. The amount of work needing to be done on a plantation was simply amazing. I guarantee you people of today would just not be acclimated to do the grueling labor required to work a plantation, and nobody would want to run one, either.

The soil composition on the Lake Bottoms was like no other on earth. It is a unique item of interest in its own right. The Lake Bottoms area soil composition was influenced mainly by the activity of the waters of the Red River. Over many years the Red River periodically overflowed, eroding and moving soils from one area and depositing them elsewhere. It was generally of a very dark clay-loam, with varying degrees of it. This was mainly the case inland of the Lake Bottoms area, some distance from the Red River. The closer to the Red River the farmland was, though, the more red it was. This was very noticeable in the area south-southwest of Wardview. The little farm area worked by Vanderbilt Wade—my uncle by marriage to my Daddy's sister Laura—was in that very location, across the road (Highway 537) from the Perry Pittman place. Uncle Van managed very well, growing cotton and corn on forty acres right next to the Red River. Only twelve of the forty acres remain today; over the years, the other twenty-eight acres fell victim to the Red River. Uncle Van also had considerable acreage near his home, in the wooded hills immediately southeast of the Lake Bottoms and slightly northwest of St. Mary. Uncle Van had one beautiful gray and white A-frame-like house setting back in those woods, which he told me he built in 1925. Surrounding the house was a cute white picket fence. In front of the house, outside the picket fence in a big, clean area was a huge oak tree. Hanging from that oak tree was the longest and sturdiest swing I ever saw, which was just one more indication of my Uncle's high quality and exquisite taste in things. I loved sitting on that swing, pushing off to a long smooth gliding motion. When my brother and I would help Uncle Van paint

Vanderbilt and Laura Wade, Early 1920s

Uncle Van held Aunt Laura in the highest esteem. He very affectionately called her "Fella." They both showed unconditional love for family and community by working hard and providing. Uncle Van worked forty acres on the Lake Bottoms and raised some cattle. They also maintained a beautiful homestead just northwest of St. Mary, in the hills southeast of the Lake Bottoms. (Courtesy of the Arthur Ford family.)

his house and picket fence we would get chased by wasps every time, and Uncle Van would laugh.

The Lake Bottoms soil was very rich in nutrients and was well managed and maintained by the plantations there. It not only grew cotton, corn, hay, and other valuable crops, but also produced some interesting-looking vines and weeds. There were two types of grass that field hands dreaded most. They were called Johnson grass and Bermuda grass. In those days, Negroes called Bermuda grass "Moody grass." Both Johnson grass and Bermuda grass grew roots that just drove you crazy. These roots grew in thick entanglements underneath the ground surface and deeper than anyone cared to dig. In the fields Johnson grass was much more plentiful than Bermuda grass. Johnson grass grew mainly in large and small patchy situations. It was one type of grass that the cotton choppers looked for as they rode the cotton trucks passed fields that needed working.

Looking at fields was part of an unwritten rating system during cotton chopping season, especially at the beginning. I would hear various comments from choppers about the condition of a field as we rode past it, for instance. Another part of rating a field was looking at the soil type and general condition. This was usually determined, at a glance, by noticing what color the soil was. The reason for that rating was because the soil texture determined how much energy and effort you were going to exert to pull the hoe through it. The lighter in color the soil, the more manageable it was. This was because it had more sand mixed in. The darker the soil, the more clay was present, causing it to be less manageable.

Once I started chopping cotton I had entered a whole new world of plantation activity, an adult one indeed, one that required mature thinking with no room for child's play. Earning a living was always at stake, and where thinking of the next day was forever important. To survive in it you needed to know how to rate fields, rows, hoes, grasses, and so on. You now probably have a better idea how and why the amount and types of grasses were the principal ways of rating a field. Furthermore, if someone among a group of people riding a truck looked at a field and said that field was "good" it meant that the field didn't have a lot of grass and the other riders would maybe turn a bit and just glance at it, feeling happy to hear and see that there was a good field, and perhaps snapping a mental image of it. Guess I don't have to tell you what someone meant when they said a certain field was "bad." They might say something like, "That field bad enough to tote a pistol." If someone said that, everybody would jump up and look with great concern and interest. But if they said, "That's some bad cotton there," people would only turn their heads and look, not wanting to end up in either one of those fields. Therefore, the condition of a field would actually set the mood or the tone of its workers for the whole day and perhaps the entire season.

When it was cotton picking season there also was an unwritten rating system. A good field was summed up in one word — "thick." If a field was said to be thick it meant that the cotton was plentiful on the stalks, which meant excellent picking and good money all in one spot. If a field were not thick, or mentioned not to be a thick field, all the workers knew they would have to pull that sack a longer distance than they cared to before filling it. It was very common for people to stand while riding a truck to get a better view of a field, especially if the field they were looking at was the one they were about to work. Making the right moves and choices when picking and chopping cotton was crucial to each day's success and survival. If you survived each day, those successes added up to survival in the big picture. I always watched experienced workers.

Experienced workers knew a lot about various situations that arose, for there was great competition even in the grueling task of working the cotton fields. This competitiveness manifested itself in tasks like selecting a suitable hoe with which to chop a row of cotton, and selecting a suitable cotton sack, in which to put the cotton, as you pick it.

Selecting a good hoe required skill, knowledge, quick reflexes, and most of all experience. During the chopping season, fields were usually worked by sizable crowds of people who had to be there and ready to start at six o'clock in the morning. They would usually arrive in tarpaulin-covered trucks, stake beds and pickups, and even an occasional former school bus. When everyone got out of the vehicles upon arriving at the cotton field, they wasted no time looking for the vehicle on or in which the hoes were brought to the field. The hoes were usually transported in a plantation pickup truck. This was the time in the morning when everyone came alive and the competition heated up. If you were lucky enough to start out the season with a prosperous plantation you had half the survival battle won right there. The other half was staying healthy and getting there. One very important unwritten code, which I always valued among the people, was to avoid physical violence. A hoe was a deadly weapon and tempers did flare. Usually a plantation worker handling the equipment would know how many heads would be there and would normally bring just enough hoes. Very seldom would any be left over. Sometimes there wouldn't be enough and more would have to be brought in. If that happened, the plantation hands got some hoes from somewhere quickly because having people stand around was a definite no-no. The hoes and their handles were of various sizes, shapes, and quality. If you were fortunate enough to be familiar with a particular group of hoes you had an advantage. And as the season advanced onward everyone would gain this knowledge, and therefore competing for the better hoes. And you can bet the grownups knew when selecting a hoe they had to be decisive and keep it moving because it was sort of a grudging custom for younger people to let the older ones make their selection first. It was kind of a pecking order that worked itself out as the days passed. Everybody would eventually learn what type of hoe they wanted and then which particular hoe in a group of hoes they wanted. They would also learn what type of hoe and which particular hoe, certain others liked. Once you learned—or determined through compromise—which hoe worked best for you, that would be the one you would look for in the pile every day. Quite often someone else liked the same hoe. If this happened several days in a row and some-one else got the hoe first, you just moved on without hesitation or complaint. But if someone happened to get the hoe you wanted, you were at liberty to exchange with them. This quite frequently happened but was usually resolved before starting time. However, everybody knew that once work started, no one was at liberty to walk away from their row without proper permission from the overseer. Once the six-o'clock-a.m.-start command was given, it was all business until the five-o'clock-p.m.-stop, or "knock off" command was given. The lunch hour, called dinner in those days, lasted from noon to one o'clock in the afternoon. At noon, when the overseer gave that command you left your hoe either standing or laying at the location where you were last chopping. An hour later exactly at one o'clock, you were back at your hoe, chopping.

There were times when a field would be finished at some point before the end of the day. At this time the workers would usually be transported to another field on a stake-bed truck owned by the plantation. These trucks had either solid or spaced sideboards. Sometimes, while riding the trucks, people would look at fields with such field-rating curiosity that everyone would suddenly be—some standing and some kneeling—on the same side of the truck, having created, in the process, a dangerous situation. I remember times when a driver would yell at riders to sit down or for some to move to the other side. Occasionally, a truck would have to stop, and the driver would get out and tell everyone to get back to where they were. Every now and then a stake-bed truck without sideboards would be used to transport workers. In this case, people would sit around the sides with their feet dangling. Being transported by truck in this manner resulted in a break in the action, which was enjoyed very much by the workers, except those who had to sit over the part where the big tires were rolling, because there they had to exert effort to hold their feet outward to keep them from hitting the rolling tires. These rides were especially enjoyed during cotton-chopping season because the pay was hourly, and the workers didn't get docked. Enjoyment and continued pay was why the transporters hurried up and got the workers to the next field.

As a plantation rule of thumb though, it was customary for workers who lived on the place to finish chopping a field or chop smaller fields so that hired hands would not have to be transported during working hours. For instance, if the crowd of hired hands knocked off just before finishing up a large field they would not be brought back to that particular field the next day. The cotton truck drivers who brought them to the plantation would already have been told to take the workers to another field for starting time the next day. That way the sharecroppers, the people who lived on the place, finished up the tedious work. But there were times when a straw boss or overseer would even handpick a few of the regular hired hands to do the work, or would have one truck of hired hands go to finish a job because the sharecroppers may have been unavailable for that chore. These types of conflicts frequently occurred during hay season, during the peak of chopping, and many times during the first several weeks of picking, when the men folk of the plantation, both young and old, were busy hauling hay.

Everything was alright as long as matters worked in the economic favor of the plantation. During the chopping season a full workday was ten hours and was referred to, especially by the hired hands, as a "day." It was six a.m. to noon and one p.m. to five p.m. in the evening. Everyone's goal was to "make a day." When the cotton trucks took people back home in the surrounding areas there would always be someone making it their business to ask the crowd, "Did y'all make a day?" or someone would single you out and ask you, "Did you make a day?" A worker would be all too eager to tell the inquirer yes, because it meant that the worker was happy to be three dollars richer for working those grueling ten hours and making that day.

Remember, the one hour off from noon to one was always referred to as dinner time. In all those years I never heard it called otherwise, and real dinner time as people now know it was called "supper." Most people had packed, or fixed, and brought dinner buckets, and as a result, used that one hour very efficiently. For instance, they would eat and then sleep until it was time to get back to the field. At the noon hour there would always be some truck going to the store, and many people, mostly the younger ones, would go and buy something to eat. The younger people would also use that time to socialize and hob nob. Yes, a few friendships and families got started from some of that socializing and hob nobbing business, even though everyone there knew they were on their own and had to stand on their own two feet. While in the fields or riding the cotton trucks, the young folks would speak two or three different slang languages, thinking they were throwing off the old folks. And I was right there in the mix. The two most popular slang languages among young folks in the cotton fields were "Pig Latin" and "Turkey Latin." Thought I was having fun talking my head off until a group of older folks laughed at something I said. After that, I totally lost interest in the "secret" languages of the cotton field crowd.

There were two popular combinations of lunchtime snacks that the younger people loved making meals of. One was a dime (ten-cent) Baby Ruth candy bar and an RC cola, and the other was a twenty-five-cent box of six big glazed donuts and an RC cola. There was something about the taste of an RC cola that just buzzed you in those days, and it had that unique burn as it passed your throat going down, to boot. There also was Coca-Cola, and Nehi with strawberry, orange, and grape flavors, all good. Pops in those days were referred to as "soda water" or "sody water," depending on who you were and who you were talking to. This was before the age of plastic bottles and pop-top cans and washed-out taste. Deposit was two cents per sody water bottle. There was a lot of two-for-a-penny stuff like candy, cookies, and gum, available in those days, and these treats were very popular. For instance, a dime would buy you so many of those big plain brown cookies that you would need a sizeable brown paper bag to carry them. It was also a time when a short loaf of white bread cost seventeen cents and a long loaf cost twenty-five cents. White bread in those days was called "light bread" in Negro culture. The older cotton choppers would usually buy a short loaf of bread and some type of bologna and sometimes some cheese, and they would normally eat up to half of their loaf of bread and take the remainder home. Sometimes bologna and cheese would be purchased and eaten with the glazed donuts, too. And, in those days a dime Baby Ruth was so big that a lot of folks couldn't eat it all in one sitting, except me, and I wanted more. Everyone always

Plantation Help Baling Hay, Early 1950s

This is the state of the art baling equipment of its time from the early 1950s. It pushes the hay right onto the wagon via a narrow chute instead of dropping it on the ground, a rarity in those days. Notice the 1940s stake bed truck in rear with farm help standing on back and someone sitting inside. Other farm help is along side and at rear of baler.
(Courtesy of the O. L. Gore family.)

managed to return to the field after dinner time (lunch) because they definitely wanted to finish the day and get paid. The straw boss would be already at, or in the field where everybody had left their hoes, waiting and looking at his time piece. The straw boss or overseer was selected by the plantation owner, and there were no questions asked. It would usually be a man from one of the families housed on the plantation. In that case a straw boss and his family and even a few kin folks would enjoy a sort of celebrity status among the workers and in the communities.

During the cotton-picking season, workers were much more on their own because the pay was by the pound—two cents per pound or two dollars per one hundred pounds. Therefore, you were on your own time and at liberty to pick cotton, not pick cotton, sleep, socialize, daydream, or whatever. But I tell you one thing, if you didn't come to the cotton field to work it would cause you to stick out like a sore thumb, and nobody cared to see that. During cotton-picking season, the typical workday was usually sunup to sundown, unless otherwise specified through notification. It took most people all day to pick one hundred pounds. A hundred and fifty pounds of cotton was considered an excellent day, and that was what everybody tried to pick. Most pickers I observed averaged about a hundred and five or ten pounds. Yet, large numbers of workers picked even less. Of course, in every crowd there was always someone who would defy all reason and probability and pick over two hundred pounds of cotton in one day. This was usually a woman. Occasionally, there was news of someone picking three hundred or more pounds in one day.

One of the most dreaded downsides of the cotton-chopping season was having no access to a toilet or restroom. I am sure field hands thought of portable toilets long before any manufacturer did. People had to walk a long way, sometimes, because of the large flat fields, just to hide behind a cotton wagon, cotton truck, or in a shallow ditch, or off in some kind of high weeds. In this regard, I remember having much sympathy for the women, for it had to be a real inconvenience for them. It was the responsibility of each hand to "keep up." That means you had to stay with the group, the flow of the crowd.

Falling behind ranked high among the reasons that an overseer would watch you closely. Some people would help others along by chopping sections in their rows. This was the norm, especially with a new hand or a family member. A working crowd of cotton choppers would maintain a team atmosphere throughout the day. I always noticed how an overseer would watch and rate the hands. Every now and then, someone would be told to not come back to work. If it were a youngster, the parent would be told to not bring the youngster back, and

when it came to an overseer, there was a zero tolerance for arguments. This is how a crowd of workers would be thinned out
to the most efficient ones. Inexperienced people were watched
by everyone for various reasons. One thing everyone admired
was good all-round workmanship. If you showed good skills
and a reasonable level of knowledge about the work and put
forth a concerted effort to perform, people would praise you
and help you along, for if a plantation had a great crowd of
workers, the talk of it would be heard on other plantations.

I saw people learning to chop cotton for the very first
time, who were being trained in chopping cotton, just take
their hoe and start chopping everything in sight, only to have
a whole bunch of people yelling at them to "stop! stop! stop!"
First of all, I would be absolutely puzzled as to how someone that inexperienced was allowed in a real field of cotton
in the first place. For instance, when I learned how to chop
or weed with a hoe, I was at home in Bolinger, working our
vegetable crops. So when I was turned loose in a cotton field,
I was ready.

Before chopping, there is a planting process. At home
in Bolinger we planted the seeds by hand. But Daddy did acquire a horse-drawn mechanical planter once. We attempted to
use it to plant our cornfield one season. We didn't make it halfway through the field before deciding that the planter wasn't
necessary, nor would it work for our method of planting. We
finished planting the cornfield by hand and never used that
thing for planting again. In fact, my brother and I played with
it just to watch its mechanical parts move. And the last I saw of
it was laying out in the grass, by the garden, with half its parts
missing. Even though a mechanical planter may be adjusted for
the amount of seeds dropped within each foot or so of travel,
it could still jam up, or malfunction, but usually worked well
if watched closely. When we planted corn at home, we saved

seeds by dropping them by hand at wider intervals to allow for easier weeding with a hoe, therefore lessening competition between plants. That way the corn would already be thinned out, thereby decreasing or eliminating the need to chop down good plants. Not so with cotton planted by mechanical planters. The tractors on the big plantations pulled four-row planters and did not skimp on the seeds. The ground would be very well prepared and the seeds usually had no problems sprouting and growing healthy plants. Cotton is ready for chopping at two to three inches high, when the sprouts have two cute little symmetrical leaves growing from the top of the stem, outward, in opposite directions. Chopping cotton involves weeding and thinning. This means you cut down all of the weeds and grasses, but only some of the cotton, only cotton plants that need to be thinned out. Your objective is to leave the plants spaced in hills or groups of one to three plants or stalks. The hills or groups should be six to eight inches apart. This eliminates or thins out excess plants, allowing for better growth of the remaining ones. It also allows for the maneuvering of a hoe between the hills or groups, which also promotes or allows for easier chopping at later dates. So, if you enter a real cotton field with the above knowledge and some practical experience you could very well be ready to earn money as an experienced worker.

Spring comes relatively early in the Southern states, especially in the Deep South. Louisiana and Mississippi are prime examples. The weather would change from winter to spring quickly. In Wardview there was year-round activity relating to the production of cotton. Plantation activity definitely moved on a strict schedule. The season's cotton had to be harvested and out of the way for winter activity, but most of all for spring activity. Winter is when much time is given to repairing plantation equipment. I remember times in December and sometimes in January, when cotton was still in the fields needing to be harvested, something which would make a plantation owner stomp his hat into the ground.

In later years, when mechanical cotton pickers started to be used on the Lake Bottoms, harvesting would be an even bigger problem because of the manner in which the mechanical cotton pickers left so much cotton behind on the stalks, hanging like disheveled locks. The mechanical cotton pickers never did a clean job, and workers were sometimes hired to clean up the fields or pick the skimpy cotton leftover from the mechanical pickers. This tended to upset the schedule of getting the cotton out of the fields and to the cotton gin, as well as the procedure of cutting the stalks and turning the ground. Before planting a field for the next season, the previous season's stalks would have to be bush hogged, or cut. A bush hog is a big heavy-duty mower normally pulled behind a tractor. A bush hog would all but mulch the stalks, which is ideal, before the next procedure of turning them under ground. It is preferable for this to be done in late fall, before Christmas, in fact. Then the ground would be turned under immediately, or as soon as possible before winter. This is done so the stalks that were turned under could biodegrade, thereby maintaining the strength of and aiding in the continued enrichment of the soil. Among the many, many things a plantation could not afford to do was get behind, for time and the weather waited for no one.

Planting cotton was done in early spring, as early as mid-to-late February or in early March. In late March the young stands of cotton usually would be (and very seldom wouldn't be) ready for chopping. If a field were planted on time it would be ready for chopping around late March or early April, sometimes even sooner. Cotton choppers all knew that it was mandatory to be ready for the upcoming season's work.

The stores, already stocked with supplies that were regularly used by workers, included hats of various types and sizes, knee pads, big pocket watches, work clothes, gloves, and more. If you worked outside in the hot sun without a hat, or even with just a little cap or other such skimpy headgear, you were definitely inviting health problems. Heat-related illnesses did claim victims. Therefore, protection from the sun was a must. In the South that is why hats were not worn just for style, but out of necessity. My brother and I would start in the spring with new cowboy hats that Daddy would have bought for us. Even though knee pads were used mainly during cotton-picking season, a few people kept them on hand to use at brief intervals during chopping season. That was because of the strain on the back from hoeing. Therefore, some people would hoe on their knees for a little distance just to get some relief from back discomfort and fatigue without stopping, usually just before or just after cutting heavy grass. All in all, knee pads were used during both chopping and picking. Most of the women, especially the young ones, wore socks on their hands to help prevent calluses from developing from holding the hoe handle. I remember thinking how funny they looked with socks on their hands, but admired their attempt to care for themselves.

During the cotton-chopping season the plantation provided at least two basic necessities. They were necessary so that workers stayed in the field chopping and not be constantly leaving in an attempt to do them for themselves. They were the provision of water for drinking and that of hoe sharpening, both for the sake of expeditiousness and efficiency. I noticed that when these two vital necessities were provided for effectively and efficiently, the workers would be in a more positive mood about what they were doing rather than displaying a more burdensome disposition about what they were doing. Water would be delivered to the work sites by pickup truck, usually by a regular plantation hand who lived on the place. The water would almost always be in a huge wooden keg with a big block of ice in it. From that big keg the "water boy" would fill his bucket. The water boy then placed a dipper in the bucket and proceeded to walk through the field to where the workers were, delivering water to each person. I can remember being able to drink water directly from the huge wooden kegs periodically. There was something about the taste of water directly from a vintage wooden keg that was to me just indescribably divine.

The hoes were sharpened by the "hoe filer," or "filer." This was a most critical necessity but was an ongoing problem because most men selected by the overseer to be the filer couldn't sharpen hoes. Sometimes the crowd would be frustrated, complaining all day about their dull hoes, at the same time the filer worked his behind off, but never sharpened a hoe. And the overseer wouldn't think of letting a young boy file hoes, no matter what the boy said. Not even the workers entertained the thought of a boy filing a hoe, thinking the kid couldn't possibly know what he was doing. And a young buck certainly wasn't going to get an "easy" job like that and get out of chopping. That stereotype was very real and none of the people gave it a second thought. Well, it was their loss. And all I wanted was a sharp hoe and in the process could have made an awful lot of others happy, including the overseer. By the time I was twelve years old I had sharpened enough hoes to chop up Bolinger. For years, at home in Bolinger, we grew a huge garden, a big sweet potato patch, and one big cornfield, and they definitely didn't get weeded by the neighbors. I learned to sharpen hoes properly from my daddy. We had about five or six hoes that I kept sharpened. Not only does a well-sharpened hoe cut razor sharp through grass, weeds, and the ground, it provides what I call a suction feel through the stroke. The feel of a sharp hoe going through grass and dirt is just something amazing. When my daddy got back on the cotton-chopping scene in the early 1960s, he was the premier hoe filer. He was in great demand. In fact, most of the people simply didn't want anybody else touching their hoes, and the overseers never argued with that.

New hoes come with a bevel that may be slightly sharpened but usually is not sharpened at all. Even if it is slightly beveled, or sharpened, it is really dull because of the small amount of angle, or bevel, it has. A hoe like this has, and will maintain, a dull disposition. It causes the hoe to dig abruptly and stop, rather than glide. So, what you want is an angle to the bevel that will cause the hoe to give you a ground-skinning, suction-like, glide to the stroke. The way you accomplish this is to cut or file a wider bevel on the new hoe without compromising or destroying the integrity of the hoe. You must keep in mind that all you want to do is alter the angle of the new bevel to a wider one, more suitable to the job at hand. You must also guard against filing or grinding off the basic hoe, resulting in changing the horizontal "straightness" of the hoe, which I consider its "integrity." This will usually take several filings unless you have a shop grinder to do the job. This widening of the angle only is in effect exactly what the non-hoe sharpeners were doing even when the angle was already wide enough from other filings. They were only widening and "shining" the bevel but not sharpening the hoe. In fact, that is what choppers would tease them about. Some of the choppers would ask the filer for a "shine." And darned if that's not what they got, which made the choppers just shake their heads in disgust. The ironic twist to the whole thing is that it is not necessarily the grass and weeds that dull a hoe, but the ground itself. The ground, or dirt, is the worst enemy of a sharp tool. And don't mention the damage caused by rocks and other hard objects.

But, even if you didn't hit a stone or something like that, the ground can be counted on to dull that hoe right up, and quick. That's the other reason why a hoe sharpener's job was secure, the imposters included.

The cotton-chopping season was long and usually lasted five to six months. The end of cotton-chopping season ushered in the new school year along with the cotton-picking season. I loved watching cotton grow from a tiny plant to a tall, leafy stalk reaching sometimes five to six feet high. Cotton usually is ready for picking in early September, even as early as mid-August. Many of us school kids earned money for lunch and other school necessities by picking cotton in the fall of the year after already having worked the fields chopping all summer. We would pick after school and on weekends. Many times workers would still be chopping after the stalks had developed growing cotton bolls, not yet opened. A greatly diminished appearance of grass and weeds normally determined when we were done chopping for the season but the maturity of the cotton stalk, with blooms and bolls, spoke the loudest. To the town Negroes who helped work the fields, the cotton-chopping season was simply done and over.

But to the sharecropper and the plantation owner the fields were now "laid by." This means that the cotton had grown and matured enough so that chopping was no longer feasible, or necessary. By this time the foliage was plentiful on the stalks, and the stalks were producing blossoms that make the cotton bolls. Also, by now the cotton stalks, with the aid of chopping, had outgrown most of the grasses and weeds, and on their own, were smothering them.

As a result, a particular field was considered finished—as far as chopping was concerned—and was therefore laid by. Sharecroppers were often happy to reach this point in the season because not only did it begin a transitional period from

Hay Hauling Chores, Mid-1950s

During the summer months the able bodied men of the plantations would be busy hauling hay. This photograph shows another piece of state-of-the-art baling equipment in those days, a bale loader in action. This particular piece of equipment is designed to pick the bale off the ground and swing it onto the wagon, for stacking by the haulers. In the 1950s this was advanced technology, so rare that most plantations were still customarily muscling hay off the ground by hand. Today there are mechanical hay ejectors, limiting this entire chore to one person. (Courtesy of the O. L. Gore family.)

chopping to picking, it also lessened the plantation's work demand and afforded the workers more rest and recuperation from the long cotton-chopping season, if only for a short time. Some sharecroppers actually experienced more off-time on weekends and evenings. It was a time to gear up for the cotton-picking season. I can remember these times putting Negro people in better moods, sharecroppers and hired hands alike. This was when people spent some of the money that they had earned chopping. For instance, school kids would have fun buying clothes, and notebooks, and other things, for the upcoming school year. Many households would purchase new cheap wood-burning heaters for the approaching fall and winter seasons. Many, many people would purchase new winter caps and jackets. So, getting crops to the stage where they could be laid by was like reaching an important milestone every year. Everyone involved would be in a festive mood. And if the plantation owner was happy, believe me, the sharecroppers would feel as though they had done their jobs well, and they would show happiness. Most plantation owners would actually reward the sharecroppers in some small way, usually in time off rather than direct financial giving.

The cotton-picking season was just as necessary to the harvest process as planting was to chopping. The first fields planted were normally the first to mature, though not necessarily the first to be harvested. And the tallest stalks didn't always produce the thickest yields. Blights and boll weevils were more destructive to the production of cotton crops than someone cutting down too many plants during chopping season. I loved looking at cotton bolls that were normal and mature. Once, I opened one—OK, more than once—and looked inside. The contents look like compacted silk. I made it a point to observe all kinds of cotton bolls that nature hadn't yet opened. I learned a lot by just checking out the growing and maturing process over the years. A healthy cotton boll is relatively large and dark green in color. They grow to almost the size of a chicken egg, with a tightly sealed point where the seams meet. You will know how many locks of cotton a given boll will yield by counting the spaces, or sections, between the seams. The ideal situation is for a cotton boll to survive unharmed to maturity and then open, revealing the contents of about four or five beautiful, thick, white locks of cotton. There are several ways to tell whether or not a cotton boll will survive. If a cotton boll is having a problem it will manifest the problem through a deficiency of dark green color and, quite possibly a smaller size. If a boll is more yellow than green it is having a severe problem and will not survive. If it is greenish yellow with brown or dark spots there is a problem. If you see a boll that appears good, but notice that it has a dark spot on it with a little hole in its middle, it has likely been invaded by a boll weevil but not yet shown the full damage. A boll like that will probably not survive. Boll weevils bore into cotton bolls and usually live in and on the contents. Any harm to a cotton boll slows or stops it from maturing.

Yes, I got hit with one of those things a few times, which hurt something fierce, and it was usually when I didn't see who threw it. Thrown by someone with a good arm, a mature unopened cotton boll could be dangerous and do some real damage to a worker. For instance, a person actually could be killed, I mean a long-goner, if they took a blast to the temple from one of those things. Realizing this, I eventually wised up and returned some fire of my own. Guess Ole Grady thought I couldn't throw. He was the stepson of the Straw Boss. Not only could I throw, I had already learned the art of throwing the things point-first while spinning. Grady apparently had a good throwing arm, because the boll he threw at me missed and cut a path in the leaves across the two rows between which, and from which, I was picking. I mean it was a real stinger, because I saw it in my right peripheral vision as it missed. I could also see the direction in which it was traveling because he threw it with such velocity that it looked like a spear cutting through the stalks. I remember thinking to myself that whoever was throwing those big cotton bolls meant to do some damage. Now Daddy had always told us not to throw things out there. I love my daddy, but there comes a time when a fella has to take a stand. At this time I was at a crossroads with thoughts of who was throwing cotton bolls at me. The question bothering me was, "Do I fire back, or don't I?" Common sense told me that if I didn't take a stand and make a statement, things would only get worse, and I felt that I didn't care to have some fool thinking he could just take his stupidity out on me at will. And

since the fool kept throwing at me, it didn't take me long to
make up my mind. Whoever it was would drop down and use
the tall cotton stalks as cover. He finally made the mistake of a
fool, and thank goodness he was missing anyway, even though
I could tell by the way that he was throwing he was trying his
damnedest to hit me. He threw a boll and I just happened to
see him as he darted down. Well, it didn't surprise me at all
who it was, because he had done some things in the past that
annoyed me, letting me know he didn't like me. It was Grady,
and he knew I had him. When he threw his last boll he forgot
to move, or just plain didn't move, to another location. When
he straightened back up I surprised him, and pleased myself,
with a shot up around his shoulder-neck area. I hit him with
a point-leading spiral that even he must have been proud of
because he never messed with me after that and I have no
memories of ever talking to him again. The plantation owner
would have stomped a few hats into the ground had he seen
people throwing the cotton bolls. I often wondered who did
the most damage to the survival of those cotton bolls, the boll
weevils or the throwers. Well, they sprayed pesticides to control the boll weevils.

    Crops were usually sprayed by airplanes. The old oil-
in-the-quart-jar method wasn't cutting it on the big plantations.
That was when you filled a one-quart fruit jar about one-fourth
full with used motor oil. Then you'd walk the middle of each
row and with your hand rake live boll weevils off the stalks
and into the jar. That was one slow and tedious process, but
perhaps safer than poisonous spray. In those days they dusted,
or sprayed from the air, mainly with double winged airplanes.
It was fun watching them fly. Sometimes when the plane flew
close you could get a clear view of the pilot's face, even though
you could already see his head from quite a distance. Some
of us would wave our hands at the pilot and he would wave

back. The pilot would focus on two flaggers on the ground. There would be one flagman, or flagger, at one end of the field that was being sprayed and one flagger at the other end, opposite each other at both ends of the same row. The flagger held a long stick, much like the handle of a hoe, in his hands. The stick had a white flag-like cloth attached to it at the top. The flagger would move the stick back and forth in a manner signaling the pilot to make his pass there. Before spraying, the flaggers predetermined with the pilot how many rows to pace off, or over, after every pass. In other words, every time the airplane flew a pass over the flaggers they would count out a certain number of rows, usually ten to twelve, and then stand there and wave their flags again. As the airplane flew over the flaggers, they would stoop or bend down in between the two rows of cotton where they were. The spray would be a dense white mist and the plane swooped pretty close to the top of the stalks. Several times, through the years, I saw my daddy flagging. I remember thinking to myself how dangerous that process must have been, with an airplane coming so close to the flaggers and the people chopping cotton. Of course, given what we know about poisonous pesticides today, the flagman method has long since been eliminated. I have been in fields as they were being sprayed. I remember it being interesting and fun to watch but I did not like it when that stuff fell on me.

The closer it got to fall, the more the foliage of the cotton stalks turned brown, drying up and dying off. By the month of November, or therein, there would be little or no problem with foliage and the stalks would be browning from lack of chlorophyll or sap. Even if the cotton hadn't been picked by Thanksgiving or thereafter, it would still be intact on the stalk because by that time the stalk would be dead, dark brown, and toughened throughout. It would stand strong and sturdy, mainly because of a huge root that continues straight

downward from the stem. This root is anchored firmly in the
ground with little offshoots extending from it. It is at this stage
that cotton is most suitable to harvest by human hands or machine, even though harvest would have begun much sooner,
not only when green foliage is still on the stalks but also when
some blooms and unopened cotton bolls are many times still
on them. Most of the leaves would have fallen off after the
stalk has dried of sap. When cotton has stood in a field much
longer than the plantation owner or manager could bear it,
they would open the field up to "pulling," sometimes even after a mechanical cotton picker had already passed through. The
method of pulling usually got a field harvested more quickly
because many pickers actually thought they were picking more
cotton and making more money because of pulling. And there
were those who simply got a thrill from being able to just put
every crazy thing in their sack. Pulling is a technique where the
space between the middle finger and the ring finger on one or
both hands is placed at the base of a branch on a given stalk,
at least one with cotton on it, and squeezed gently. Then you
slide your hand away from the stalk toward you, capturing everything on that branch in one motion. Whatever was on that
branch is what you put in the sack. Word of mouth spread the
news fast when a plantation was pulling. Of course it didn't
take me long to figure out what the down side, or catch, was to
that one. In other words, when the weigher put the sack on the
scale and knocked off enough weight from the total to make
you sick, you knew what the deal was. And there was nothing you were going to do about it. Thereafter, pulling did not
impress me and was never again included in my activities. In a
pulling situation you more than likely lose, and that was definitely done in favor of the plantation. I wonder if they knew
someone would be opening up those cotton bolls to see how
they looked inside? Or, maybe they knew some of us young

guns would be having cotton boll wars, costing the plantation money. Guess we were bound to pay somehow.

When harvest or picking began, all the appropriate farm equipment was brought out and set up at the field that was about to be picked. One or more cotton wagons were brought to the site, depending on the size of the crowd. The wagons were normally pulled by tractors. In those days cotton wagons were constructed of wood, except for the wheels and tires, of course, and much of the running gear, or undercarriage of the wagon. The bed and side boards were normally constructed from a durable hardwood. These were the more inexpensive rough cut boards obtained directly from a saw mill. The wagons were usually well constructed and reliable because they were used for many chores around the plantation, like hauling hay. Anyway, when a wagon was brought to a cotton field for loading it also served as the weigh station. The weigh station consisted of scales and a "P" or "Pee"—a counterweight, which completed the weight-measuring apparatus—and was supported by a strong board attached with nails or wire to the top portion of the wagon's rear, sticking out about three feet. In later years, the pull-down weigh scale became popular. The weigh station is where the workers brought their cotton filled sacks for weighing.

On the weekends, usually on Saturday, the picking crowds were quite large. There would be lots of young people who attended school during the week. There would be people from towns and settlements east, west, north, and south of Wardview in attendance. This was normal procedure, however, for a huge cotton plantation located in those days along Highway 3 between Benton and Bossier City. There were people you knew and people you didn't know, for anyone could pick cotton. All it required was reaching and getting it. Parents would have little children out there with pillowcases and

croaker sacks, otherwise called burlap bags. In fact, throughout plantation history, especially during the years of slavery,
this itchy, rough, scratchy, dense cloth also resembled the cloth
used to make clothes for slaves, particularly field hands. It was
commonly called "nigger cloth." This type of plantation terminology continued well into the twentieth century, used by
old folks in the cotton fields and at home, where it was tradi-
tionally passed through the generations.

When cotton sacks, the manufactured ones, were
brought to the field by a plantation hand on a truck or wagon,
the delivering party would throw all the sacks on the ground.
The sacks were of various lengths, sizes and quality. There
would be new ones, old ones, some slightly used or broken-in,
and some very used. Some were tar-bottomed. This is a sack
with a coating of tar on the bottom of it from about the halfway point of the sack to the rear end of it. Experienced cotton
pickers knew what kind of sack they wanted. Their selection
was determined by several factors. Who was weighing, for instance, determined whether or not you took a tar-bottomed
sack. If the weigher was known for knocking off a lot of
weight you wanted a tar-bottomed sack so it would be worth
it. If the weigher was generous and didn't knock off much,
all you needed was a good long sack without tar, because he
would only knock off closer to what the sack might have actually weighed. Tar-bottomed sacks provided an excuse for some
weighers to knock off more weight than they perhaps should
have, whether it was an old sack with almost all the tar dragged
off or a brand new one with that really thick coating on it, they
would knock off the same amount. Some weighers had a strict
policy of knocking off five pounds for tar bottoms and some
knocked off more than five pounds. I have seen as much as
ten pounds knocked off for a tar-bottomed sack if the weigher thought it was also wet from dew or rain or had excessive

Mechanical Cotton Picker, 1962
This original model of a mechanical cotton picker is shown in action on the O. L. Gore plantation, operated by Philip Thomas. This machine was manufactured in the late 1950s and is shown here in the early 1960s. (Courtesy of the O. L. Gore family.)

dirt or mud on it. Dealing with tar-bottomed sacks and overly ambitious weighers were just some of the hassles of picking cotton for the workers. If you were dealing with a cheating weigher, especially one who made it clear that he had no regard for people who picked cotton, you would want to limit your trips to the scales. If the cotton was thick you wanted a long regular sack so you could pack it hard and tight, all the way from end to end. I have seen a good, long, well broken-in sack net over a hundred pounds. That was a rare and exciting thing that all plantation help and workers wanted to witness in their time, whenever possible.

Once the man threw the sacks on the ground, people would rush them. If there were not enough sacks, someone would have to wait until more sacks were brought out. You didn't want to be left without a sack, no matter how you picked. Whether you picked fifty pounds a day or two hundred and fifty pounds a day, you would be in one embarrassing situation if left without a sack. First of all, you're wondering how you did not get even one sack from a huge pile of sacks that was on the ground. And there you are, thinking, standing around burning daylight and losing money while others are already picking cotton and making money—and laughing at you. Cotton sacks have a heavy-duty cloth loop, or strap, that goes over the head and around the neck of the picker. The upper part of the open end of the sack near the picker was cut higher so that it would fit close to the picker's body under the dominant arm, the arm the picker uses to put cotton inside the sack. And the outside of the upper part of the sack was cut lower to allow the dominant hand to enter the sack more easily. Whether the picker was right-handed or left-handed, the same sack worked either way. All the picker had to do was loop the sack's strap over the left shoulder for right-handed picking or over the right shoulder for left-handed picking. After selecting a sack you wanted to select a row, or two, that allowed you to be as close as possible to the weigh scales. And some people actually carried three rows while keeping up. You don't want the first two or three rows in the field because their growth is usually stunted. There would usually be someone there, for whatever reason, to jump right on those short rows. So you won't have to worry much about that. All you have to do is watch experienced workers, who will likely have the same thing in mind as yourself. The closer you can stay to the weigh station, the shorter the distance you'll have to carry your full sack. I always noticed how women had a knack for getting men to carry their full, heavily-packed sacks to the scales. If a field had a large crowd, there would be a weigher on the ground and a full-time sack-emptier on the wagon. During picking season the weigher was usually in charge of the workers when the crowds were not huge. The weigher would have a log book or a piece of paper where the names of all the people who weighed cotton—or had someone else weigh it for them—were entered. Every time a worker brought cotton to be weighed, that weight would be logged by the weigher next to that worker's name, unless the weigher was otherwise instructed. When the day ended, everyone gathered to be paid, usually right at the scales. The weigher stood next to the payer, usually the plantation owner, and called out names. The entire crowd of pickers would be conglomerated there, being very quiet, observing the action. When a name was called, that person stepped forward, slightly within two arms' lengths of the payer. This "not getting too close" was a very real and traditional custom. In those days, getting too close to a white person was considered "crowding" them, which they considered threatening. The weigher then told the payer how much to pay the person. The payer then counted out the money and handed it to the person. The owner, or payer, went strictly by what the weigher said. If there was a dispute you had to prove your claim. To prevent that from happening, the trick was to communicate all along, ensuring the weigher logged your proper weights as you visited the scales. You had to make sure you saw the weigher enter the proper weight, because at the end of the day, whatever the weigher said went, and was accepted by the payer. Otherwise, it would be quite a task to prove the weigher wrong. And the plantation owner was definitely not prone to tarrying there.

The more cotton you got in a sack the better it was, as long as you were stout and strong or had another way of getting your sack to the scales. For instance, if the weigher were in the mood for knocking off five pounds per sack that day, and you didn't have a tar-bottomed sack, and you visited the scales three times, when your sack wasn't even close to full either

Weigh Scales and "P"

These scales were used for weighing cotton in the South. They are exactly like the ones used in the cotton fields of Bossier Parish. These particular scales were purchased in an antique shop in the state of Indiana in the mid 1990s. The dealer said that he and his wife purchased them while traveling in the South. (Courtesy of the Arthur Ford family.)

time, that's fifteen pounds of weight taken and the sack itself may actually weigh three pounds. That way the plantation had you eat six pounds for the day. Let us say there were fifty workers who had that type of sack and weighed cotton three times that same day. Averaging among fifty workers resulted in three hundred pounds of cotton picked free. On the other hand, there was talk of pickers cheating, adding weight-enhancing substances to their sacks of cotton. The only time I knew of a foreign object being put inside a cotton sack was when a huge unopened cotton boll or a stone would be placed in one of the bottom corners of a sack by the plantation for weighing purposes. A strong piece of wire would then be wrapped on the outside of the sack around the cotton boll or stone in order to secure it in the corner. The wire was then looped to form an eyelet. This eyelet was what held the bottom end of a sack on the scale hook as the sack hung on the scale to be weighed. The top, or front end of the sack, was supported on the scales by the sack strap, which sometimes would be hung first. But in all the years I worked the cotton fields, I never knew of or witnessed anyone putting anything other than cotton in their sacks. At any rate, six pounds translates to twelve cents out of your pocket, when you would have been lucky in the first place to clear two dollars the whole day, even without mishap. There were far fewer people picking one hundred thirty pounds than there were picking one hundred pounds.

Sometimes you had to empty your own sack; this was usually the case with men and boys, especially if the crowd wasn't very big and there would only be a weigher at the scales. That would mean extra time spent away from picking your row. The emptier's job was to pull the sack up and over the side boards with a boost from the weigher or someone else, normally the person who filled or brought the sack to the scales. The women normally were not held to this unwritten custom. Sometimes a sack would be packed so full and tight like a log that it would hardly bend to be scaled. When people managed to pack their sacks like that they would be the object of complimentary teasing. Such as, "Where you get that log?" Or, "Wish I could pack mine like that." Sometimes the tight packers would carry an extra, smaller sack of some type with them, mainly the women tight packers, so that when the big sack became too heavy to keep dragging while picking, they would leave it and keep picking, using the small one. Then when they got an impressive amount in the small sack they would walk back to the big sack and empty the contents of the small sack into the big sack. They would do this until they had as much as they wanted in the big sack. I tried that once, lost my concentration, got confused in the process, wondered why in the world I was doing it in the first place, decided it wasn't worth all that, and never did it again. So I just kept pulling the heavy sack. Besides, people would steal from the sacks of other people, and I wasn't about to leave a big sack of cotton way behind, unguarded, laying there for the taking.

Fields of tall cotton stalks were havens for rogues, tricksters, and deceitful persons. No matter who you were, there was always somebody willing to take from you. For instance, dinner buckets got stolen during chopping and picking. Someone would eat the contents of your dinner bucket and place the bucket back where you left it. You had been out there all morning thinking about how good those biscuits and potato salad and that fried dry salt meat were going to taste. Now you're suddenly wondering what kind of world you live in, because you just opened your dinner bucket and discovered it was empty. Then you start to blame yourself, for how you should have known better than to leave it unsecured in the first place, and so on. It is also stuck in your mind how you had just learned another expensive lesson. Now you've got to go through the rest of the day feeling your big guts trying to eat up your little guts, while at the same time trying to figure out who ate your dinner because everybody there was going about as though they didn't eat your food, and nobody had left the cotton field. Then, after you start to adjust and go on, you start to wonder what your next expensive lesson is going to be, and when it is going to be, and where you are going to be when you experience it. Guess that's what I get for living in the Brier Patch. In the Brier Patch you are always hearing about how some people can steal baking powder out of a biscuit. Now you know.

When the wagons filled with cotton, they were ready to be taken to the cotton gin. Wardview had a cotton gin. The main part of Wardview was a crossroads, or four corners. The cotton gin was on the northwest corner. C.A. Rodgers' store was on the northeast corner. A lesser-known store was once located on the southeast corner with some residents beside it to the south. And Joe Rich's store was on the southwest corner alongside a huge cotton field that stretched far south along Highway 537. State Road 537 ran west, from Bolinger, off Highway 3 to Wardview, and vice versa. It was a black-topped road that was well traveled in those days. In Wardview, State Road 537 intersected with Arkansas Line Road, which ran north. At that time the blacktop of State Road 537 West ended just past the cotton gin, just west of the four corners. The dirt portion continued westward toward the Old River, about a quarter of a mile, dividing a couple of cotton fields along the way. Along the dirt continuation of the road, just past the cotton gin to the west, stood a church in the corner of one of the cotton fields. Across the road from the church, on the south side of the road, in back of Joe Rich's store, was a house with a relatively small fenced-in lot with some cows in it. But State Road 537 itself turned south at the intersection in Wardview and ran all the way to Miller's Bluff Road, turning left there and proceeding to Highway 2.

During the entire cotton harvest season, from September to December and often in January, the cotton gin buzzed with harvest-related activity. Wagons of cotton were staged under huge sheds near the cotton gin, waiting to be emptied. Watching the gin worker empty the wagons was interesting. A wagon would be pulled under a port like a lean-to and stopped beneath a huge pipe-like apparatus that was long, vertical, and flexible at the top and could be moved back and forth. This pipe served as a vacuum. The worker held on to the vacuum by handles attached to it maybe three feet from the bottom. This is how I saw the wagons being emptied, and I figured the vacuum system to be a smart way to ensure that the cotton would enter rather clean and separated. Every time I took a few minutes to stand anywhere on the four corners and just look at that cotton gin, I would reflect on how it all happened, from start to finish.

Harvest season, especially at its peak, was a very busy and demanding time and the cotton gin could always be heard running in the distance. It brought on a need for extra storage accommodations for picked cotton. All the plantations did the same thing to alleviate the problem. They would do it because wagons would be in short supply, in use, or "tied up" in many ways. Some would be at the cotton gin loaded and waiting to be unloaded. Some were being used for gathering more cotton for transporting it to the gin. The cotton had to be taken out of the fields, and if there were no wagons available it would be held in temporary shelters. These shelters, called cotton houses, included several kinds of buildings, including old empty houses on the plantations, where sharecroppers once lived. Some were very old and permanently vacant, and some were temporarily vacant. Sometimes a family moved into a house previously used for cotton storage, whenever it was vacant and needed. There were times when cotton was also put in huge piles on the ground and covered somehow, usually with tarps. Barns also provided space for cotton storage. But my favorite cotton houses to observe were the portable cotton houses. These houses were built on long wooden beams serving as slides. They would get moved to different areas of the fields for the sake of convenience and availability. They had large hinged lids on them that were like a one-sided pitched roof or much like today's metal trash dumpsters, but much larger. They were very interesting, economical, and adaptable to different situations. Sometimes weigh scales would be installed on a corner of these temporary cotton shelters, much like on a cotton wagon, and sacks of cotton would be brought directly from the fields by workers to be weighed and emptied inside them. The gathered cotton then remained in the shelters until wagons became available to transport it to the cotton gin. Cotton harvest season is normally finished anywhere between

Thanksgiving and Christmas. Many of the wagons would then be tucked away under storage sheds or inside barns. Most of the fields were then prepared for turning.

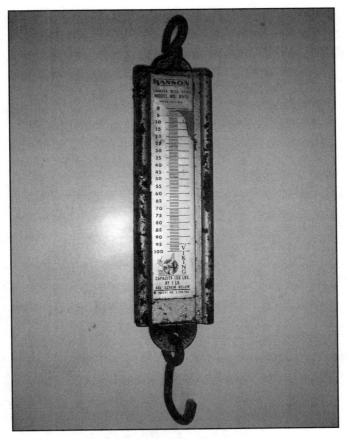

Weigh Scales

This pull-down type scale was becoming popular on cotton plantations in Wardview starting in the lower mid 1960s. This unit was made in Shubuta, Mississippi. It was purchased in an antique shop in Indiana in the mid 1990s. (Courtesy of the Arthur Ford family.)

Wardview, Louisiana
(also called the Lake Bottoms)

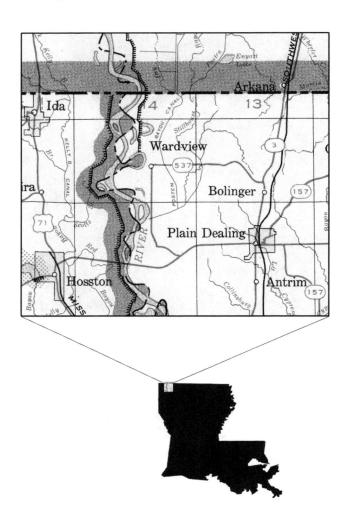

CHAPTER TWO

Sharecropping on the Lake Bottoms

The plantation system was strict and rigid, and obviously only possible when someone did the work. It took a certain type of individual to own a plantation; it took a certain type of individual to work a plantation; it took a certain type of individual to enslave another individual. What I find phenomenal is that these and other events culminated at a point in time that rivals the occurrence of the age of Aquarius, the lining up of certain heavenly bodies of the Universe, the signs of the Zodiac, a true coming-together of happenings in world behavior that resulted in the creation of a system on which the whole world has no doubt come to rely. The whole world has come to rely on us, the United States, because of the wealth and stability of life that we maintain, which obviously and undoubtedly has been possible because of slavery in our country. The United States is still very much a Mecca for people of all nationalities, religions, ideologies. Stability in the world as we know it—economic, social, religious, and otherwise—always came at a price, that which few among us care to admit or deal with, the price of human exploitation and the sacrifice of lives. The effects, or the ripple effects, if you will, of slavery in the United States still abound and are yet felt all too well by the descendents of those who suffered enslavement.

What does it tell you when foreigners can come to the United States, acquire businesses, business properties, residential land, and other valuable American assets in just a short time, and prosper? What does it tell you when descendents of slaves invest time, hard-earned resources, and endless struggles and hours of preparation, and then lose out, only to end up wondering, "What happened?" Now, the descendents of slaves constantly end up back on the bottom economically and psychologically strapped and are now faced with pulling themselves up again at home, in the United States. What happened? What happened is that the world beat a path to one door, but made sure it stayed away from the other door. When slaves in the United States had to pull themselves up from that position of humiliation, it cost everyone, especially the slaves, in every sense of the word. First of all, the struggling slave was not trusted, a problem that is still confronted by their struggling descendents; not trusted by their neighbors, their neighborhood businesses, or the world at large. And worst of all, the struggler was, and still is, blamed for his own predicament, even when so many other forces beyond the struggler's control came in to play to help cause the predicament. Blame was put on the victim by the masses of peoples of the world from the beginning and has been passed from generation to generation, all generations, through socialization of all types, and teachings of all types. Just as slaves passed along information to their progeny on human indignities that they endured, which affected their lives, survival, and existence, descendents today talk about how foreigners discriminate against them upon their arrival to America, as though they were already prejudiced. Therefore, how can you be judged objectively by someone who is already prejudiced against you? So, collectively, the world does not beat a path to your door.

The people of the southern United States believed so strongly in their way of thinking that they thought they could disassociate themselves or secede from the Union, which they themselves helped build, forfeiting everything and becoming self-sufficient and independent. Did that take some guts, or what? As it turned out, it did require intestinal fortitude, as well as an extreme case of tunnel vision; however, it still had to be attempted. It took me a while to realize, though, that some people will try anything, as long as they can coerce or force, someone else to pay the price.

As the great families of the Lake Bottoms survived from one January to the next, their existence reflected a cycle in the rhythm of human existence worthy of documentation, even though practically all of this valuable history remained ignored and largely undocumented. This selective amnesia exists because most who endured it felt it was a shameful way of life, and they thought other people should not know about it. This, in my opinion, played right into the hands of the oppressors, for if they could squelch what they were doing, nobody "on the outside" would ever know. I call "great" any family that survived on the Lake Bottoms; but to exist on the Lake Bottoms as a way of life, a family tradition, generation after generation, is almost beyond comprehension. The great Lake Bottoms families that stand out in my mind are the Browns and the Littles, just to name a couple. Somehow, families like these mastered the lifestyle of the institution of sharecropping, also known as "batching" to some, even while sometimes working relatively small tracts of land that they owned. Other families that came and went measured their sharecropping performances by the standards set by these families. I can remember Momma and Daddy talking about how much cotton the Browns had picked at the end of a given year. I also remember us all being happy one year because we had equaled the total cotton-bale output of one of the highly productive Brown families. Even though the Browns had a reputation for not liking to be outdone, I remember them as polite people. Some of the younger Browns went to Carrie Martin High School, as we all did in later years. I remember Vader Brown. Vader V, as we called her, was a cute, dark-skinned girl for whom I had a lot of respect. We were in the same classes for a while. She had a beautiful smile; I liked looking at her pretty teeth when they were revealed by her confident smile. I admired Vader V the most for her solid personality and wonderful integrity. A family of Browns moved to Bolinger for a brief period of time across the woods, less than a mile from us. We had fun belting out echoing harmonies across the woods to each other at night. Caddy Bryant, a member of another mainstay Lake Bottoms family, was a singer and leader of the noteworthy Hearts of Harmony gospel quintet, with whom I traveled and played guitar when I was a teenager. In those days the only musical instrument that accompanied this type of group was the amplified or electric guitar. Any other instrumental accompaniment was rare. The singers of the Hearts of Harmony were very professional, and we rocked those country churches.

Sharecropping, or batching, was the epitome of plantation competition. When you understand it, you will see why. Sharecropping sounds like a good thing, people helping people. Maybe in theory. I don't know of any Negroes who were happy with that situation, and their movement in and out of it manifested a distaste for it. In reality, sharecropping was more like a clever continuation of slavery. The idea was for the plantation owner to get the work done at little or no cost to the plantation, while at the same time making a family of workers think they would be paid fair and square for their work. The plantation owner took a family whose hand had been forced, who were at their rock bottom, and sold them a dream. The family had to take it because they were in the Brier Patch and had nowhere to go but up. You see, when a family was sharecropping, no paychecks were coming into the household. That type of allowance was so rare that it was unheard of, and unknown to most. The sharecropping family had to buy everything they needed, normally on credit, and usually from the plantation resources—from food and clothing to housing. Ac-

cording to plantation custom, nobody was to worry because
everything would be "settled" at the end of the year. However,
at the end of the year, things too often became quite a different story. Most families were promptly informed by the plantation owners that they owed the plantation money. Somehow,
most plantation owners were good at deflating something that
was already deflated. These were among the many reasons why
Negro workers would seek to work for a plantation owner who
demonstrated a reasonable level of integrity year after year. A
few plantation owners did actually have reputations like that.

The plantation division of labor fell on the backs of
the sharecroppers. The families would be assigned many different chores. Some were responsible for working certain fields
in designated areas of a plantation, usually starting with the
ones surrounding, or near, the plantation houses in which they
lived. This way, they could walk right out of the field and into
their house to eat their midday meal, and that would save transportation time, which most sharecroppers did not have anyway.
A small distance from the house, beside the field, stood their
outhouse for toilet purposes. Telephones and television sets?
Forget it. Not on your life, not in those days and under those
circumstances. Sharecropping was all about plantation chores,
and maybe reading the Bible. Sharecropping, in our time, involved a five-and-a-half to six-day workweek with only Sunday
off. On Saturday, most sharecroppers worked either the whole
day, depending on the urgency of the chores, or a half-day,
which ended at noon. During the cotton-chopping season, everybody, including the trucked-in help, placed a premium on
Saturdays off. Chopping cotton was much like hauling hay; you
had to do it while the sun shined. Even to get half a day off on
Saturday was considered a special treat, so you could connect it
with Sunday, which you knew you already had off. Of course,
with sharecropping, time off depended on plantation priori-

ties. When sharecropping you had to make yourself available when needed, twenty-four hours a day, seven days a week. And plantations always had work getting behind, emergencies, and some quick special chore somewhere, night or day, needing to be done. Therefore, sharecroppers relaxed and claimed a little pleasure whenever or wherever they could. Social and other activities occurred mainly on weekends and some weeknights— for those who could manage them—for evenings and nights were occupied figuring and planning for the next day's chores, and most of all, resting and sleeping.

Sharecroppers, especially those on a given plantation, usually knew each other and socialized together sometimes, but not with white folks who might be working on the place. The order of segregation of the Lake Bottoms didn't allow for the mixing of Negro and Caucasian sharecroppers. Jim Crow law maintained a rigid form of racial segregation that kept Negroes and whites from mingling. When white folks worked in the fields, it seemed as though they were smuggled in and smuggled out. They didn't work the fields necessarily as a way of life and never in large groups. Of all my years working the fields, I remember seeing a white family working some distance across a field from us maybe three or four times total. On every occasion it would be just one family, and we would never know who they were. There would be a whole lot of staring, on both sides. The talk among the Negroes was that they just did not believe what they were seeing, but were impressed to see it because that made them feel like white people might work too. One established rule of the segregationists in the South was to make sure that poor white families didn't fall through their safety net and land on the Negroes.

In the early to mid-1900s, people of the Lake Bottoms managed to establish at least two public schools for the Negro people of that area. One was called the Lake Port School, and the other was called the Still House School. The Lake Port School was located near the "Port of Wardview," as I call it, where bustling ferry activity once provided travel services for the people of settlements like Mira and Ida, Louisiana, west of the Red River, who moved to and fro across that portion of the Red River, all the way from antebellum times to the mid-1900s. This was just a stone's throw from where the western portion of the O.L. Gore property is across the levee today, and near where a portion of the Lawrence Horneman place was back in the day. Wardview did have its own port, which received goods and supplies from points mainly south of there, including Shreveport. The waters of the Red River have long since claimed a huge portion of the land that supported ferry, port, and plantation activity in that area. The Still House School was quite some distance from the Lake Port School. The Still House School was located in the northeast corner or region of the Lake Bottoms area, not far from, and just south of, the Arkansas-Louisiana state line. The Log Ferry Road provided public access from the southern and western portions of the Lake Bottoms to the northeast area of the Lake Bottoms. This road crosses what was formally known as "The number one Ditch." This huge ditch was dug across the Lake Bottoms to serve as a drain for flood waters. It started at Log Ferry Bayou in the northeast portion of the Lake Bottoms and meandered southwestward before emptying into the Red River, in the southwestern portion of the Lake Bottoms. The people of the area called it, then and now, the "Big Ditch." This Big Ditch is well over a hundred feet wide in places and once required a log ferry for people to cross. Riders operated the ferry by pulling on a rope. This same ditch crosses Highway 537 twice, east and south of Wardview. Of course, the only thing missing today is Wardview itself. And how I miss Wardview. Instead of ferries crossing the Big Ditch today, there are various bridges lending solid footing to travelers. One acre of land was donated for the Still House School by a prominent Negro couple of the area, Paul and Nina Burney. They owned and worked ninety acres of land there. The school was built by the Bossier Parish school system. It was a sturdily constructed two-room building, of which the remains of the frame and foundation still stand today. It was added to, enclosed, and used as a hay barn after the Burneys sold their farm and moved from the Lake Bottoms. The two colored schools were rivals in sports. The athletes walked the distance between the schools. White students throughout the entire Lake Bottoms-Wardview area attended the Plain Dealing High School in Plain Dealing, at that time a twelve-grade school for whites only. They were already riding buses to school. Carrie Martin High School, a twelve-grade school for Negro students, was eventually built in Plain Dealing, which spelled the end for the colored schools of the Lake Bottoms as well as other one- and two-room colored schools in other parts of Bossier Parish.

On the Lake Bottoms, a few churches stood in the corners of cotton fields. For recreation, Negro families gathered, especially on weekends, and played baseball and other games, many times in cow pastures. June 19th was widely celebrated by Southern Negro people. When I grew up in the South, I was so aware of June 19th being celebrated by Negroes that I never got around to asking anyone why, and no one there ever told me why. It was after I left the South when I found out why, and was simply amazed. Guess it was one of the many history lessons Mr. Wright taught us that I forgot.

Wardview hosted bear wrestling contests in those days. After our family moved to our permanent home in Bolinger, we once attended one of the bear wrestling contests in Wardview. It was one funny sight, seeing the bear jerk the men around, making the men's hair swish about on their heads. I did hear about how one man out-wrestled a bear once by applying a bear hug. Some people would go and fish off the banks of the Old River and maybe the Red River too, but most people started staying away from the Red River, especially after the bridge connecting east and west Red River banks along Highway 2 was built, which helped eventually bring ferry activity in the Wardview area to an end.

I don't know whether that Red River was jinxed or haunted, or what, but people just stayed away from it, all except me. I use to walk over to the Red River all by myself because I just couldn't squelch the memories of people talking about the horrors of the Red River. I couldn't stand not knowing the truth any longer, so I had to go. Even in the later years of my youth when we lived in Bolinger and were trucked back to the Lake Bottoms to work the cotton fields, I would steal away to the banks of the Red River. As you can see, I made other use of that midday hour we got off during chopping season when I wasn't sleeping.

When we worked the fields near the rivers I would walk across the sunken area where the Red River had meandered long before. There grew the tall cottonwood trees with their silver-bottomed leaves that I loved to watch flicker in the wind. Standing on the high bank, I had a giant's eye view—almost a bird's eye view—of them, and they were simply a precious sight to see. After I got my fill of looking at the trees once again, I went down the steep bank and across the stand of cottonwood trees until there it was. I could see and hear the waters flow, but most of all I went there to see if the falling banks story was true. It was true. I stood there watching the west bank. As far as I could see, in both directions was a cliff-like, straight-edged, red dirt embankment. The red banks were void of vegetation. It wasn't a high, mountainous cliff, but it did rise quite a distance above the water level. I could hear an occasion-

al splash but was determined to actually see it. My eyes kept
scanning that awesome bank until I saw something I would
never forget. Suddenly, at about the one o'clock position, there
was a huge, vertical, column of red dirt, peeling away from the
bank. As it peeled away, I remember how the immediate open
space behind it appeared temporarily dark. Without crumbling,
it fell right into the water, giving off a majestic splashing sound
captured by my ears and a unique sight captured by my eyes,
and then only reluctantly passed along to "the ages" of my
mind. For years, both before and after we moved from Wardview back to the hills and continually hearing stories about the
banks of the Red River falling in, I remember, as a kid, worrying that the Red River might swallow up the Old River, then
Wardview, and then work its way to Bolinger. But I guess the
Red River decided to direct its meandering ways to the west of
Wardview, instead of cutting eastward. Of course, I eventually
got over that fear, but I never forgot the sight of the falling
banks of the Red River.

There was a levee that ran from the northeast banks
of the Old River all the way north, and possibly beyond, the
area of Half Moon. I don't remember Half Moon as a town
or sizeable settlement. It consisted of a few homes and some
pretty big cotton fields of the O.L. Gore plantation, centered
around the existence of a banana-shaped river named Half
Moon, also known by the Negro people as Half Moon Bay. We
worked the fields in that area, but nothing much north of that.
I saw some cattle but mostly cottonwood trees for some distance, which told me that the waters of the Red River flowed
there. Wherever there were cattle alongside the levee, their pastures were guarded by fences on both sides of the levee. So I
felt relatively safe from the dangerous bulls that roamed the
pastures, keeping them replenished with mainly the Hereford
breed of cattle. Of course the Brahman bull, in the South

called Brahma, was the most feared, for they seemed naturally aggressive. They were on the Lake Bottoms in small numbers, but dominated the pastures of the Bossier Parish hills. The levees were built in those days by the Army Corps of Engineers, not only along the Red River, but along the Mississippi River, north and south, to safeguard nearby lands and private properties from rising flood waters of the mighty rivers. When I was

Paul Burney, 1892 – 1977

A one time property owner and resident of the Lake Bottoms, Paul, with his wife Nina, owned and worked ninety acres of land there. They donated one acre to the Bossier Parish Schools, on which the Still House School was constructed. Even though a subsequent owner added to the two-room structure and used it as a storage and hay barn, the basic school building foundation still stands today with some solid walls and two original chimneys. (Courtesy of Mr. Judge S. Burney.)

a youngster, I thought the levee on the Lake Bottoms was just a long hill with cows near it, and on top of which plantation owners drove their pickups and had fun. I was a very inquisitive fellow and asked questions. So, when someone told me the levee was constructed to keep the Red River from taking over the cotton fields, it eventually started making sense.

The levee, running north from the Old River, also dissected a portion of the Lawrence Horneman plantation. This is where we once stayed. Another family also lived on the Horneman place during our time there. They were the Bradfords, a polite family, who I thought got along very well with Momma and Daddy. I remember our family living in an old shotgun house on the east bank of the Old River, on the corner of a Horneman plantation cotton field, an area accessible only by a little dirt lane. This lane, running directly off the Arkansas Line Road just north of Wardview about half a mile or less, was well traveled by pedestrians and farm machinery. We then moved across the levee to the north bank of the Old River, on the levee's west side. The area of the Horneman place west of the levee was accessed by Horneman Road, a graveled dirt road that ran right up one side of the levee over to and down the other side to the darkest, most isolated part of the Lake Bottoms in those days, which I always thought of and referred to as "down behind the sun." It epitomized our world of oblivion. The graveled dirt road was accessed from the south by the Arkansas Line Road, traveling north from the four corners of Wardview, perhaps a mile. All that was over there were a few plantation houses and a big plantation barn, surrounded by cotton fields. The barn stood alongside the graveled dirt road on the north side of it just over the levee, west of it, which is also where the quality of the graveled dirt road abruptly ended, just past the barn, but continuing westward toward the Red River as a one-lane road. This was the road that accessed the

Nina Burney, 1899 – 1956

Nina was the wife of Paul Burney. She was a devoted housewife and notoriously talented seamstress. She earned money by designing, sewing and repairing clothes for the public. (Courtesy of Mr. Judge S. Burney.)

Port of Wardview many years earlier but became less traveled after the Red River claimed the land where the Port was once located, as well as a portion of the Horneman Plantation property years later. Alongside the road, just west of the barn, was one of the plantation houses. And in front of that house, directly across the road, was another plantation house. So, in that little area there were two plantation houses and a barn. The remaining plantation houses on that side of the levee were south of where these buildings stood, at the south end of the large cotton fields. This is where my family and I spent our last days and nights living on the Lake Bottoms. On that side of the levee, what stopped the cotton fields on their south side was a sandy dirt lane that hugged the Old River atop its north bank, much like the sandy dirt lane that ran along the east bank of the Old River where we had lived before. Like the Half Moon River, the Old River was shaped in a semicircle, like a sickle blade, or the sickle-shaped moon at night, thus, Half Moon.

The Horneman's place had mainly shotgun houses for sharecroppers to live in. These houses were constructed with a hallway down the middle and rooms on both sides. The hallway was three feet or so in width. It ran straight from the front door to the back door. There would be two or three small rooms on both sides of the hallway. The houses accommodated families of different sizes. These houses mimicked the double barrel shotgun, for which they were named, with the empty hallway down the middle and loaded rooms down both sides. Hardly any of the plantation houses in those days had electricity, and the toilet was a small outdoor building across the backyard, near the cotton field. People usually avoided going outside at night though, for fear of snakes and other dangers. At night, for toilet purposes we used "night buckets," as they were known in public, but privately called "slop jars." The slop jar would normally be kept in Momma and Daddy's room until it needed to be emptied, but the front and sides of the porch also got their share of night time activity.

The plantation houses we lived in never had electricity while we were in them. We lived by the light of the oil lamps at night, and the light of the sun in the day. Moonlit nights were a treat for us children, because we could play outside. In the run of a year there weren't a lot of moonlit nights, so playing with the lightning bugs was a big event for children. When the sun went down we would start getting ready for bed to rest for the next day's plantation work, since we had to rise early, before daybreak. Bedtime was also when the family would get their talking done. Some of us would go right to sleep, others would tell a story or share some information they had heard in the cotton fields. Sometimes we children had to be told to hush and go to sleep. I remember sleeping on pallets all the time. A pallet is a quilt or blanket or an old coat or something similar spread on the floor, on which to sleep, usually without a pillow. If there were a bed in the house, it was considered a special blessing—just short of a miracle, really. None of the other plantation people could give you anything because they, too, had nothing. The only wood we could scrounge up had to be used for cooking so Momma could fix a dinner bucket. Momma would make biscuits and fry dry salt meat and make potato salad to pack in our dinner bucket. She packed the food in an empty lard bucket. Many times that was all we would have to eat the whole day. The dinner bucket was a real drawing card. It brought every family member from the house to the field because they knew that was their one chance of getting something to eat. Usually, when other people would be working the same field as us, Momma would have us keep the dinner bucket out in the field with us, for we could not afford to lose our food. Most of the houses had peach and persimmon trees growing around them, which also provided food. We didn't have any hogs on the Lake Bottoms because there was nothing to feed them. We acquired hog meat when Daddy helped someone else slaughter their hogs, usually some of the "established" sharecroppers who were mainstays. On the Lake Bottoms and in the hills, Negro people would get together and slaughter hogs in the late fall. Winter survival of families was heavily dependent on that meat. This is why hog stealing among Southerners was just a no-no. As long as I can remem-

ber, hog stealing was a "death sentence" of sorts, if someone
was caught at it. Every part of a hog was used after it was
slaughtered. Some people even made hogshead cheese, not a
dairy cheese, but meat with spices.

When we lived on the Lake Bottoms, I didn't know
telephones existed, or televisions either. We slept with doors
and windows wide open, and nothing bothered us. I remember watching the moonlit waters of the Old River sometimes.
When the nights were so dark and stealthy, I remember many
days dreading to see the sun go down because of the lonely,
frightful darkness. I liked walking the sandy dirt lanes along the
river banks during those days, feeling my bare feet sink in and
at times throwing clumps of dirt and sticks. I liked looking at
the trees and grasses and weeds along the banks, studying their
differences and noticing how they insisted on growing side by
side in seemingly perfect harmony. Nighttime usually started
with everyone working at staying off each other's nerves, because there we were with no place to go. My siblings and I
learned to trust Momma and Daddy's judgment, because they
were all we had. If we had to go anywhere, we walked. We relied on Momma and Daddy for safety and comfort. We often
went to sleep by the sounds of their voices. The most responsibility plantation life put on us little ones was to just follow,
stay out of devilment, and do as we were told. Our lives on
the plantation were just not centered on traveling, visiting, or
having fun. At that early age, I sensed that we were in a life or
death struggle. On just about any given night someone could
be heard crying themselves to sleep. I was no exception, being
only four years old at this time. This was the beginning of my
discovery that I had to be a fighter, if only because I just didn't
know how to give up. Besides, I had started realizing at that
early age that my work was most definitely cut out for me and,
because of it, decided I would not be denied. For some rea-

son I was destined to blaze trails and live on the cutting edge, whether I wanted to or not.

When we moved away from the Lake Bottoms, it was sudden to me, and without notification. I don't remember anybody talking about the fact that Daddy and Momma had hired someone to build us a house in Bolinger. That explained why we spent the hard times sharecropping on the Lake Bottoms. That also explained why Momma and Daddy had to hurry and buy that land and building materials with the money that Daddy, in later years, told me he sent to Momma from Richmond, California, where he worked for the Ford Motor Company. He told me the money was getting spent fast. That explained how sharecropping was costing us, instead of paying us. Before my family moved permanently into our Bolinger home we had worked most of the Lake Bottoms. I was there as a little fellow, but before I was eighteen, I had been trucked back to work the cotton fields of the Lake Bottoms for years. In fact, I had the unique experience of having worked portions of the entire Lake Bottoms area. If only for my sake, Momma and Daddy had to get that house built quickly or I just might be having the unique experience of sharecropping to this day.

CHAMPIONS OF WARDVIEW

Some of the Farm and Plantation Owners of Wardview's Lake Bottoms:

O.L. Gore
Jeff Morgan
Alton Keoun
Lawrence Horneman
Bob Boggs
Duke Pittman
Dave St. Clare
Milton Pittman
Pete Hilliar
Perry Pittman
Cliff Lowe
Fouty Gardner
Jimmy Davis
Homer Sullivan
Charley Rodgers
Roy Morgan
Ben Winham
Harry Wilson
Henry Cox
Tom Stevens
Denson Barnett
J.W. Lee
Joe Rich & Bennie Rich
Madie King

CHAPTER THREE
Champions of Wardview

I hope you now have a better understanding of how Wardview impacted the lives of so many people, all types, including sharecroppers and plantation owners alike. Herein is an impressive list, for honorable mention, of many of the plantation and farm owners who came and went through the unique area of the Wardview system. This list was originally handwritten and given to me by Mr. Odie Lee Gore, Jr. He said there were four or five more names that he could not think of at that time. I was well aware of, and a witness to, there being several different plantation owners on the Lake Bottoms, but even I didn't know there were that many. What an important piece of historical information this is. Some of those named in the list I actually knew in those days. There are also names of men I knew, though I was unaware then that they had farms on the Lake Bottoms. This list of names serves to demonstrate how the Wardview area of Bossier Parish was a Mecca for so many people caught up in a struggle for survival, so many families visiting, if only for brief periods in the passage of time, and making their unique contributions to the sustenance of life in that locale. The one name I added to the list was Perry Pittman.

This chapter focuses on two families of Wardview in particular, one representing the sharecroppers culture of the Lake Bottoms and the other representing the plantation owners activity of the Lake Bottoms. They are both worthy of representing this chapter of Louisiana history and both still have family living on the Lake Bottoms of Bossier Parish—near where Wardview was—when all others have come and gone, even Wardview itself. The Littles represent the sharecroppers and the Gores represent the plantation owners. There are none better to represent their respective sides, and I was there and will forever be their witness. The Littles were so productive at sharecropping they managed to acquire and work over two hundred acres of their own land. The Gores, on the other hand, gained the reputation among Negroes of being fair and decent plantation owners, who openly showed appreciation for the Negroes who worked for them. I remember all this and believe it is no wonder that both families still survive on the Lake Bottoms. I found that the common denominator between these two Lake Bottom families was the great strength generated by their love for family and their respect for home and community. I always believed that these qualities were the virtues binding together all the people of Bossier Parish in those days, and these traits produce winners every time. That is why I call them the champions of Wardview, and both families come from humble beginnings.

The Little family in those days centered on Willie and Hester Little. Their livelihood was based on a parcel of land located along the north side of Highway 537, just east of Wardview. They were well situated for convenient access to the cotton gin, stores, church and other community accommodations, for life on the Lake Bottoms revolved around the production of cotton and the cotton gin activity in Wardview. There were many fishing places, the main location was the Old River. A church along Highway 537, across the road from the Littles, was built in honor of the matriarch Mrs. Little. They named it Hester's Chapel, which is discussed later. With all the necessities of life, as it was defined in those days, available in and around Wardview, some people rarely left the area.

Before moving to sharecrop on their own, Willie and Hester Little lived and sharecropped with her father, Wes Cole, who had moved to the Lake Bottoms from Minden, Louisi... Ben Little, Willie's father, was also from Minden, Louisiana. Having left Wes Cole's place, Willie and Hester moved to the place of William George and sharecropped for one season, or one year, and then moved on to rent the Cliff Lowe place, which consisted of forty acres, for six years. Since money seldom changed hands in those days, under those circumstances, the Littles rented the Lowe place for portions—fourths,

Hester and Willie Little

Miss. Hester, as everyone called her, and Mr. Bigon, as everyone called him, were so productive on the Lake Bottoms that people simply thought of them as omnipresent. They mastered the art of sharecropping, performing with machine-like precision in all their pursuits and taught their children to do like-wise in life. (Courtesy of the Little Family.)

osed to "standard rent." This means the
ourth of whatever the land produced. For
ed cotton, every fourth bale was theirs;
every fourth bushel was theirs. So they
ve place for fourths." They earned money
from the Lowe place and bought a farm of two hundred and
forty acres, on which, by the way, the cotton gin of Wardview
originally stood before it was moved to its final location on the
northwest corner of Wardview. The Littles made a good living
from those two hundred and forty acres of land, until they lost
the parcel to foreclosure, due to lack of flood insurance and
the damaging flood waters of the Red River. The flood of 1935
on the Lake Bottoms had forced their hand. Obviously, they
never gave up. As a result, Miss Hester resumed sharecropping
with her father, while her husband Willie and their son John
sought work elsewhere. After John came of age and served
time in World War II, he returned home determined to help
his parents get back on their feet. He always thought they were
heaven-sent and decided to help them acquire some eighty
acres, even though he was no longer interested in farming and
made that known to the family. Shortly thereafter, John moved
to Minnesota to live and work. Mr. and Mrs. Little managed to
keep and work the eighty acres with their other son, Raymond
T. Little, whom we all called "Bim." In addition to helping
her husband maintain their land and family, Hester Little also
worked outside the home. She was very influential in the insurance and mortuary business through a company in Minden,
Louisiana, from 1936 until she died in 1970. During her years
of service to the general public and her community, Hester
Little championed many positive changes in burial procedure,
record keeping, and policy writing for the benefit of everyone,
not only the Negroes of Bossier and other Louisiana parishes.
And it was widely known that her number one supporter was

her husband, Willie D. Little. Miss Hester, as everyone in the Negro community called her, was so dynamic that a church she founded was named in her honor. A perfect historical accounting of Hester Chapel was given to me by Mrs. Margaret Little Haskin and also presented in the program for a church service on October 16, 2005, commemorating the seventy-third anniversary of the church. An excerpt from it follows below:

> The Hester Chapel C.M.E. Church was founded in 1932 by Hester Little with the assistance of her husband Willie Little. It was organized from Sunday School classes being taught in the home of Ophelia Thomas, Mother of Hester Little. Several Phelps Lake Bottom families were involved in the organization of the church because they had no transportation to their respective churches. Among the families were: Brothers Macon and Ephraim McCauley, Charlie Little and Jessie Robertson. As the church grew, others came. Among them were: Brothers Webb Bankhead and Lee Green as well as Sister Cornelia Bennett.
>
> As the church grew and prospered, Reverend W.M. Thomas [w]as assigned. They moved from the house into a storefront. Under his leadership, one acre of land was purchased and a brush arbor was constructed as the first building on the newly purchased land.
>
> In 1937 Reverend J.M. Ellis was assigned to serve. Under his leadership, the first framed building was partially constructed. Financial problems prevented completion. Services were held in the incomplete edifice until the condition was such that it was unsafe to occupy the building. The Deacons of Pilgrim Rest Baptist Church offered the use of their church allowing Hester Chapel to continue services until another church could be constructed.

Over the years (between 1944 and 1956) hard times prevented rebuilding to the satisfaction of its founder. The flood of 1945 destroyed most of the materials needed to continue construction. Under the leadership of Reverend J.J. Cornelius and Elder Leroy Alexander, the church was reframed. For a short period of time, school was held in this incomplete structure. Later, Reverend L.W. Smith became pastor and plans were made to install a new roof. Being determined to build a church structure that would last long after she was gone, Hester Little became even more determined to build a stone church [.]

In 1956 Reverend Anderson Heard was assigned to pastor Hester Chapel. Under his leadership and the determination of the founder, the current building was constructed. As other pastors were assigned (Rev. M.C. Lewis, Rev. Odis Taylor and Bishop Gilmore) more improvements were made. The floor was raised and water and bathroom facilities were installed.

In 1970, Hester Little passed away. There were those who were determined to continue the work that she had begun. Her daughter, Georgia Little Webb was encouraged to take the reins and continue the work. She, too, had a dream for Hester Chapel. She dreamed of air conditioning, padded pews, a piano, choir loft, pastor's study, finance room, and a fellowship hall. With prayer, determination, and the pastoral leadership of Rev. Delores Williams, the Dream Came True! . . . .

Thanks be to God for all that He has done and for those who came before us leaving this church as a beacon in the community.

So, if you opt to travel on the Lake Bottoms of Bossier Parish don't forget to notice Hester's Chapel, right across the road from the original eighty acres that served as home for the Little family of Wardview.

I will never forget that fall day around 1953 in Bolinger when Momma and Daddy and we children were all sitting on the front porch eating watermelons and spitting the seeds wherever they landed. Up the little lane leading to our house walked the figure of a man. He walked right up to the low end of the porch, feet still firmly on the ground, and sat down on the porch. Nobody stopped eating watermelon. This man wore khaki pants and a white shirt. He greeted all of us very politely. I thought, what a nice man. Momma and Daddy obviously knew who he was because my Momma spoke up and said, "How you, Mr. O. Lee?" At that time, I was between six and seven years old and had not remembered hearing Momma and Daddy speaking of the man. He greeted my parents, "Hello Mozel, Hi Lump." And they proceeded with their talking. I remember the man watching us younger ones move about. My baby sister, Mary, was about three and a half, still wearing diapers, and cleaning up on the affections of us all. The man said to my Momma, while looking at Mary, "Mozel, y'all must be doing alright 'cause every nine months I come up here y'all got another one." All of us laughed at that. He had come to ask Momma and Daddy to work for him. I came to know of this great man as Odie Lee Gore. As I grew older and worked the cotton fields, I heard other field hands mention this man's name. The Negroes referred to him as "Mr. O-Lee-Go." They always said favorable things about this man. Because he did solid things with his plantation on a consistent basis throughout the years, and because his plantation is still in operation up to this day (though mainly as a ranch now), Odie Lee Gore

Odie L. and Sylvia Gore's Original House

This is a far cry from Frank Lloyd Wright's designs but think of the great Americans that humble beginnings have produced. (Courtesy of the O. L. Gore family.)

Little Odie Gore, Jr. or "Sonny," with Jesse Alexander

O. L. Gore, Jr. is shown here as a toddler with Jesse Alexander. Jesse is weeding the garden. Junior grew up and became a formally educated man and runs the Gore place today. (Courtesy of the O. L. Gore family.)

could very well be crowned champion of the Lake Bottoms.

Odie L. Gore and Sylvia Cobb were joined in holy matrimony in 1922, approximately two years after Gore began farming forty acres of land. Gore built their first house at that time. In keeping with their hands-on tradition, the Gores did everything that plantation life offered, including actually working in the cotton fields on a regular basis, which is good reason why the Gores saw themselves as farmers rather than plantation owners. As the years progressed the Gores managed to acquire over a thousand acres of land. Despite almost annual floods in the formative years, the Gores still managed to work all the land they acquired. One of the worst floods in Lake Bottoms history occurred in 1945. This flood covered the entire Lake Bottoms area, all the way to the hills on its eastern perimeter. These and other flood waters prompted O.L. Gore to go to bat for all the people of the Lake Bottoms by writing letters to state and other representatives concerning the damaging flood waters of the Red River. He got results when others did not even try, thinking that efforts of that sort would yield no positive results. The Gores were so family- and community-oriented that Sylvia Gore many times gave people food to eat when they stopped and asked for it, on their way to wherever, while walking past the Gores house. And Mrs. Gore even stepped up and managed the plantation whenever necessary.

A Negro man named Jesse Alexander lived and share-cropped on the Gore plantation for thirty-five years. He was allowed to work a small portion of the land for himself and was actually paid a monthly allowance for his efforts. He spent lots of his time helping the Gore children. Even today, O.L. Gore, Jr. speaks with great appreciation for Jesse Alexander because Jesse played a major role in grooming him for running the plantation.

In 1945, when the big flood came, O.L. Gore noticed a little dry spot of land as they paddled by in an old Cypress boat. It was the only dry spot around and Mr. Gore predicted that he would build a house on that dry spot, which he eventually did. It turned out to be Sylvia Gore's dream house, built of pretty red bricks. The house still stands today and is as pretty as it was the first time Mr. and Mrs. Gore laid eyes on it.

Today Odie Lee Gore, Jr. operates the plantation and ranch. Sonny, as family and friends call him, is a pleasant man with an outgoing personality. He is married and very proud of his family. Sonny is a perfect example of someone displaying the many factors that are necessary for the longevity of a plantation and family. I will discuss this and other reasons why the Gore plantation survived on the Lake Bottoms, while many others succumbed to its brutal ways and fell by the wayside. Mr. Gore shared valuable information with me about their plantation, from its early years to the present.

In my wildest dreams I never thought that the entire Wardview/Lake Bottoms area could be flooded by the Red River, but I learned from Gore that it was. And to think, this area was huge enough to host several plantations. After viewing Gore's aerial map of the Wardview area I could clearly see how flooding from the Red River was all too possible. Viewing the map finally put together the puzzle of comments I heard through the years about the Red River. Gore showed me the area where the Red River consumed seventeen acres of their plantation property. The force of the meandering waters is mighty and for years was influenced by a damming process some distance northwest of the Lake Bottoms area. An aerial view of the area shows how Old River and Half Moon River were formed. The mere shape of these two rivers tells me quite a story. In brief, they were both, once upon a time, even perhaps at different points in time, themselves part of the Red

Odie and Sylvia Gore

Odie Lee Gore, Sr. and his wife, Sylvia, were the driving force that kept the Gore plantation operating through the ups and downs of life on the Lake Bottoms. (Courtesy of the O. L. Gore family.)

A Hands-On tradition

This photo is just one more that proved all the Gores were not afraid of work. It shows Sonny (Odie, Jr.) with some of his cousins picking cotton with a smile. From left to right are Malcolm, Francis, Sonny, and Mary. (Courtesy of the O. L. Gore family.)

Family Activity

This photo shows Odie and Sylvia Gore sharing some fun chores with family and relatives. They are cleaning fish and entertaining some nice fat chickens that insist on hanging around. Mr. Gore is kneeling with his back to the camera while Mrs. Gore is in action at the right of the group. (Courtesy the of O. L. Gore family.)

Walter Gore and family – 1912

This scene shows Walter Gore, fourth person from left, accompanied by his family and his mules. This is a typical plantation work depiction of that era involving a hands-on family. Notice O. L. Gore, Sr. as a young fellow sitting on a mule in right-side portion of the photo. (Courtesy of the O. L. Gore family.)

River. And the fact that the two rivers are virtually identical in shape clearly indicates meandering, which, in geological terms, means only the Red River could have established those bodies of water. Hundreds of years ago, perhaps two thousand or more, these and other bodies of water remained in the area established by the meandering ways of the Red River, thereby creating the area "The Lake Bottoms," particularly Phelps Lake.

It is very interesting indeed how the Gore plantation came to be. It did not start with Odie, Jr., nor did it start with Odie, Sr., though he did do an amazing job of consolidating the operation. The Odie L. Gore plantation started with a dream that was passed along. That honor goes to a man whose love and dedication to his family and community stood the test of time. Because of those virtues, this man challenged the destructive ways of the Red River, and groomed his posterity accordingly. This man, Walter Gore—referred to as "Papa Gore"—came from Ida, Louisiana. O.L. Gore took the reins from the hands of Papa Gore, and inevitably, O.L. Gore, Jr. was bound to follow. Ida, located west of the Red River, near Arkansas, hosted a cotton gin at that time. Walter Gore lived in Ida, Louisiana, with his family, but ferried back and forth across the Red River at the Port of Wardview, near where the O.L. Gore place is today. The Port witnessed a flurry of activity by many inhabitants of northwest and southwest Bossier Parish, as well as persons from places in southwest Arkansas and northeast Texas, such as Texarkana. So one can see how the Port of Wardview was a very busy place. Odie Lee Gore obviously valued and built upon the concrete philosophy of Walter Gore, survival-oriented, with confidence and optimism as he went about his daily endeavors, focusing on farm, family and community. While people like the Hatfields and the Mc-Coys were taming the mountains of Appalachia, people like

Walter "Papa" Gore, 1924
(Courtesy the of O. L. Gore family.)

Walter Gore and Children – 1928

This picture shows Papa Gore sitting atop his favorite riding horse holding two children, Margaret and Wilma. (Courtesy of the O. L. Gore family.)

Cotton field being worked by mules

From the looks of the stalks this field of cotton is being prepared to be laid by. Notice the blooms on the stalks in the foreground. There are three two-mule teams, one handled by each man. O. L. Gore, center, is doing the same work as his help. (Courtesy of the O. L. Gore family.)

Walter Gore were taming the waters of the Red River, very much like my Daddy in taming the timber of Bossier Parish. Among all these great Southerners were "mountain people," "river people," and "timber people."

When Walter Gore dreamed of plantation ownership and wealth, he was smart enough to know that he lacked resources and "elbows." So he did exactly what the great swing band leader Benny Goodman did. It is interesting how these men nearly paralleled each other and in totally different lifestyles. Goodman surrounded himself with masterful, swinging Negro musicians like Charley Christian on guitar and the great Lionel Hampton on vibes; he maintained that tradition, and the rest is history. Walter Gore surrounded himself with master Negro farmers like Richard Jennings and taught his son, Odie Lee Gore to do the same with the likes of Jesse Alexander, and to this day Odie Lee Gore, Jr. is no exception in that regard—and the rest is history. One mark of a great manager is knowing he can't do it alone, and thereby developing the art of knowing how to put the right people in the right places and making the right survival choices. On the Gore place today Ray Montgomery, Linell Parish, and the Odie L. Gore, Jr. family are making it happen.

The Old Home Place

This picture shows what Odie, Jr. and Glenda Gore, his sister, called the old home place. What is even more interesting is the bonafied cotton field in the foreground ready for picking. (Courtesy of the O. L. Gore family.)

My Favorite Picture

This picture shows Odie, Jr. looking like a proud little man. He is eagerly showing his favorite calf to Mary, for it is the thought that counts. I can appreciate the old car and the house that was so lived in by wonderful people. The Gores lived in this house until 1964. (Courtesy of the O. L. Gore family.)

CHAPTER FOUR
Early Family Heritage

There was a time when I was a boy I actually thought maybe the sun rose in Bolinger and set in Wardview, or somewhere on the Lake Bottoms. Well, it's a good thing I never asked anybody. What I mean is, I always saw the sun rise in the east over our cornfield and always saw it set west of our house, behind the farthest trees I could see. I knew that the Lake Bottoms area was over there and I associated that locality with being "down behind the sun." Of course, this was after we had left the Lake Bottoms.

Our family actually lived in Bolinger before we moved to the Lake Bottoms in the late 1940s. The first Bolinger house burned down when I was six months old. You are probably wondering how I know what happened when I was six months old. I know because my oldest full sister, Maude, would not let any of us forget, especially me, all the way up to the time she passed on to Glory. All my other sisters at home at that time gave the same accounting of what happened. Momma had gone to fetch some water from someone else's well and had told the girls not to go outside the house. She had left a fire burning in the kitchen stove, out of which a piece of flaming wood fell onto the floor. The girls said they watched the fire engulf the kitchen and when it became too intense they ran to the next room and huddled together in a corner. When the fire spread to where they were, they ran to another room. They kept that up until they ended up on the front porch, huddled near the front door. Maude was a couple months short of six years old, and my other sisters were even younger. While the

Mozel and Arthur "Lump" Ford
They married and raised their children in Bossier Parish. Worked their way as sharecroppers through the Lake Bottoms and settled in Bolinger. They were both very productive and represented their Southern heritage well. (Courtesy of the Arthur Ford family.)

younger girls were running from room to room, Maude was miraculously saving me. She always explained it the same way. She said the fire was rapidly advancing. I was lying on the far side of the bed close to the wall kicking and screaming my head off. She would always remind me how she had the sense to pull the sheet on which I lay very slowly because, she said, she knew that if she had pulled it too quickly I could have rolled the opposite way and wedged between the bed and the wall. Maude said she gently pulled the sheet toward her until I fell into her arms. Then out of the house she ran, passing the other girls huddled on the porch next to the front door. She said she yelled to them to come on. They all then ran down the steps and a few paces onto the front yard. Maude said they looked back and the burning house was falling in. She said it made an awful sound. It was quite a deed my sisters pulled off that day. The burning of the house is what forced my folks' hand.

We then moved to the Perry Pittman plantation on the Lake Bottoms. Momma and Daddy sharecropped there a few years and then moved to the Lawrence Horneman place for a briefer stay. We lived on the Lake Bottoms, sharecropping for about four years. Shortly before I was five years of age, we moved into our second house in Bolinger, which became our permanent home. I remember we used coal oil lamps before we had electricity in our new house, as we had done on the Lake Bottoms in the old plantation houses. During the time when we burned oil lamps in our new house in Bolinger, I can remember the dim, flickering flames that seemed as though they lit up everybody's face. A woman Momma called Sus Kelline would visit us often during those days and some of the nights. She greeted our family the same way every time. She was very polite and always said kind things to us, and would look straight at me, saying with a smile, "W-h-a-t-a b-o-u-t the

W-h-i-p-p-o-o-r-w-i-l-l, J-u-u-u-n-yah!?" Early on, I must have
said or done something about the Whippoorwill to start such
a tradition. When Sus Kelline would ask me about the Whippoorwill, everybody, except me, would laugh. Even though I
never understood why everybody thought what Sus Kelline
said was so funny, I must admit I was quite fascinated at what
she said and how she said it. The only conversation I remember having about the Whippoorwill was as a little one, I asked
Momma what the bird was saying. What my mother said, and
how she said it, will stay with me forever. She looked at me
smiling and said in a beautiful, dramatic voice: "June, he sayin',
Chip!, Flew out the White Oak!" I remember thinking that was
an awfully smart bird, knowing that chips fly. Of course, now I
think of the majestic manner she used to comfort the inquisitive mind of a child. It was very believable and fitting to me,
because not only did the bird actually sound like that, but for
years I had watched my Daddy make chips fly from fallen trees
with our axe, which in turn taught me to do the same. And
since the bird stayed in the woods, I thought it always watched
us and wanted to tell us what was happening.

   Our permanent house faced south and stood on a plot
of land slightly less than four acres, right across the road from
where the other house burned down. In my youth, I used to
see the sun as a guiding light, my Guardian Angel indeed. It
became the yardstick by which I measured the progress of
each precious day. I learned to follow its every move. Watching the sunrise became a must for me; besides, life in the rural
South demanded that you get up and move it. There was no
such thing as oversleeping. And what was amazing is that we
didn't have alarm clocks. Maybe the folks in Shreveport had
them. In the country, you had your five senses and you either
developed and used them, or you perished. When the sun rose
above our cornfield on the east side of our house, it was a sight

Permanent House in Bolinger

This post 1965 photo of the house in Bolinger, Louisiana was taken in 1988, three years after Daddy died. For years I plowed the area where trees have grown and are visible in the right side of the photo, on the east side of the house. It was a corn field an acre or so in size. (Courtesy of the Arthur Ford family.)

to behold. It was fiery red and looked as though it were dancing. The dew on the corn stalks glittered from the light of the sun. At times, I felt compelled to walk to the edge of the cornfield and rub my fingers across a wet leaf of a corn stalk and watch the water collect in the middle of the stalk. Every time I wanted to daydream while working, the sun would somehow seem to get my attention and remind me that time was passing and nothing was getting done, which in my situation in those days meant wasted time. When your work is cut out for you, time is of the essence, simply because you already know what you need to do. Therefore, productivity meant the world in the rural South. For instance, if you didn't grow your food, you didn't eat because there was little or no money with which to buy food. So when the sun would let go of me and set over the faraway trees, I wanted to be able to say to myself that another day's job was well done. And at the end of the long summer days, when the horizontal background of a dim reddish-pink sky silhouetted the dark trees at twilight, was when the Whippoorwill sang.

I was born January 21, 1947 at Charity Hospital in Shreveport, Louisiana, in Caddo Parish. I eventually learned that Charity Hospital was a special place for colored people. I would hear the older people in the cotton fields talk about that hospital. If someone were fortunate enough to make it to the Charity Hospital it would be the talk of the fields, for even in those days there were babies being born in old houses. One of my life's desires was to go to the Charity Hospital and thank them and let them know that they had done a good job.

Shreveport is located on the west side of the notorious Red River, and Bossier City occupies the east bank. Even though the Barksdale Air Force Base in Bossier City was an important economic engine for the entire Bossier City-Shreveport area in those days, cotton was still king. Louisiana has always been known for its huge cotton plantations, which were plentiful in most parts of the state even though sugarcane and rice were also produced in great quantities. The South has constantly beat out the cadence by which our whole nation always so gallantly marched. The United States of America was able to make giant economic leaps because of the exploitation of free labor by African-American slaves. I always thought of America as living on slave royalties, just as it was meant to be by some people.

Southern Negroes' lives were more intricately woven into the fabric of the Confederate way of life than most Negroes, and others, would care to admit, and at the same time, the slaves passed historical information down through the generations. My Southern heritage tells me that the Confederates weren't fighting just to make sure that slaves remained slaves. They fought for the land because it was home, livelihood, and family. The land was Southern survival, and Southern Caucasians thought of the enslavement of Negroes as a right. So the Confederates embodied the epitome of a people fighting from the heart, with all they had. And what they had was their land and their slaves. I heard many of the older people in the cotton fields talk about things that happened in "de ole slaby times" as well as in the Civil War. While growing up in Bossier Parish, I knew of several people who were well over 100 years old, and according to their family members, all they could talk about was slavery and the Civil War. One such individual went by the name of Webb Bankhead. During the Civil War, Negroes were skillful horse handlers, driving them hooked to supply and ammunition wagons, and were also responsible for scrounging up and preparing food for either cause, Confederate and Union. Civil War battles, skirmishes and other activities occurred in many parts of Louisiana, even along the Red River. There were battles fought on the eastern side of the state, along the "Mighty Mississip," the Mississippi River, which divides most of Louisiana and Mississippi. The Civil War ravaged the entire Southern economy. Negro men fought in the Civil War as soldiers and worked in the Civil War as servants. From start to finish, Negro slaves served in the Civil War as servants to their owners, and as servants to the sons of their owners. Negro labor built forts, dug trenches for battle, and built breastworks, vestiges of which still stand today in some of the preserved Civil War battlefields. Negro servants also had the responsibility of making sure the dead bodies of their owners and other military family members of their owners arrived home safely for burial. Southern Negroes, free and enslaved, contributed numerous tangible goods to the Civil War effort, including

money. Southern Negro Civil War veterans were told not to
talk about their experiences in the war and were denied pen-
sions by the CSA. These are only some of the reasons that
all Southern people were adversely affected by the Civil War.
Civil War reenactments are usually very well put together, but
they are presented from a limited standpoint as far as the racial
makeup of the participants. Documented proof of this can be
found not only in military records, but also in personal letters
written home to loved ones by Civil War soldiers, both Negro
and white. I do believe that if one were to go to such great
length to tell a true story, it would be enlightening to all people
to represent everyone involved. In every American war on record, due recognition of the Negro soldier has always been a
national problem.

The winds of the Civil War still blew strong when I
was growing up in the South. There were people who were
very frustrated with the situation, but mainly with the effects
of the Civil War, whites and coloreds alike. It would have been
difficult to find someone that the war didn't break. We had
become even more dependent on the land and ended up with
even less to work with. It was a common thing to hear the
old Negroes talk about how they would hear white folks still
curse "that damn Sherman," meaning General W.T. Sherman,
blaming him for single-handedly setting fires and pillaging
the South. Kizzie Root, the mother of most of our grown-
up neighbors was an old, well-preserved, tough-minded, nice
Negro woman who lived just up the road from us. She still
talked about Marse (the master), and how he fed them parched
corn from a trough. In the South, we had to figure out and
create ways to move forward, while at the same time consol-
ing and supporting posterity. I saw many old people, colored
and white, who had inherited what I call the Civil War stare.
Folks on my Daddy's side of the family had it. The stare is

a placid, emotionless one where the eyes pierced your presence, seeming to reflect events of the past, memories of which lay deep inside them. These kinds of people usually didn't say much and went on their way as though their minds were made up about something, never to be altered. Many times I would say something or do something that would open them up and even sometimes make them laugh. It was a wonderful feeling watching them act as if they were being relieved of some heavy burden. There was something I was asked so often that I could sense when it was coming: "Ain't you Lump's boy?" Something all the old folks wanted to know, if they said anything to you, was whose family you belonged to. Sometimes that would be the only thing they said to you.

My grandfather Milton Ford was born in 1858, three years before the Civil War commenced. He was my Daddy's father. Daddy was born in 1898, according to a family document I prize, even though Daddy insisted he was born in 1899. I figure that's close enough, but at the same time, I realize that one year can make a huge difference concerning many things. My Daddy, Arthur Ford, was the tenth of thirteen children born to Grampa and Gramma. Their first child was Uncle Willie Lemon, born in 1881, and their youngest was Uncle Elve, born in 1904. Family and others knew Grampa's name was Milton and called him "Milt." On the records of Louisiana land deeds in Benton he is erroneously listed as Melton Ford. Grampa Milt was just a little fellow when General Lee surrendered to General Grant at Appomattox, Virginia, and when President Abraham Lincoln was assassinated, he was seven years old. Grampa was of mixed heritage. He was raised by a man name Henry Thomas and his Native American wife. Grandmother, Daddy's mother, was from Tollette, Arkansas, a settlement named for the Tollettes. Her name was Lucrecia Tollette. She was Native American and everyone knew her as

Milton Ford, 1858 – 1927

Grampa Milt, photographed here at the Louisiana State Fair in the early 1920s, was one proud man who never ceased showing it, probably because he was married to Gramma Lucrecia. Well known in the entire Bossier Parish community he was quite active therein. He was very influential among many prominent residents of Bossier Parish such as the Hugheses, Matlocks, Malones, Hudsons and many others. Milton Ford was well based in community services, civic and other. (Courtesy of the Arthur Ford family.)

"Aunt Lou." She was a true matriarch and, in my opinion, a saint. Grampa and Gramma were married; they lived on and worked thirty-five acres of land they owned in Red Land, a settlement adjoining Bolinger on the east, located a short distance northeast of Plain Dealing. These three settlements are several miles northwest of Rocky Mount, Louisiana.

The Hughes family of Rocky Mount was big in early Louisiana state politics. They hosted a secession meeting in 1860 at their Rocky Mount house, which is featured in the historic square in downtown Benton, Louisiana. My Daddy's family, the Fords, were very well known and respected by the Hugheses, Matlocks and Malones, among many other families I heard him talk about. Grampa was a God-fearing, God-cursing, industrious son of a Caucasian. Daddy told me about two fine mules that Grampa owned and with which he worked his crops. That would be like owning two big farm tractors today. I always noticed that people tended to exhibit behavior that would take years to understand when their survival depended on the land. I, along with some other field hands, saw a plantation owner stomp all the good looks out of his hat once. Southerners tended to do that when something failed to meet their satisfaction. Of course, we saw so much of that kind of behavior that we figured out it was more show than impulsive emotion. When they got done stomping hats though, there was no question as to who was in charge. Daddy told me Grampa earned money, but was a hot-headed man who needed Gramma to keep him in line. Grandmother Lucrecia was like a well of hope and wisdom from which more people than just our family drew thirst-quenching water. Her light shined wherever she went. Grampa died in 1927, and Gramma died in 1930. My mother's father was born in 1895, and he was one restless man. Momma told me he had a good job on a train. She said he quit the job and started riding the train. Everybody called him Poppa John. Poppa John lived in the vicinity of Pocatello, Idaho for some years. He was also of mixed heritage, mainly Native American. He moved around quite a bit throughout his life and lived to be ninety-four. Poppa was indeed a rolling stone.

My mother's mother was of the Layton family of Bossier Parish; they were of African-American descent. My mother was born in 1919 and was raised by her Aunt Mammie Layton, whom we called Grommau. Grommau was a clean, motivated woman and was highly opinionated and dedicated to her way

Lucrecia Tollette Ford
Native American, Born Antebellum – Died 1930

Lucrecia Tollette was the wife of Milton Ford. She was from Tollette, Arkansas, a settlement named for the Tollettes. The Tollettes were known to be stern and very community oriented. Aunt Lou, as people called her, was religious and believed in the general welfare of everyone and proved it by her life's performance. (Courtesy of the Arthur Ford family.)

of thinking. She went to church often, saying she was saved because she didn't want to go to Hell. Of course, now, Grommau was ready to fight if you disagreed with something she said or even if you offered another point of view. Grommau lived in Plain Dealing in a modest little house on the south side, down a dirt road in a quiet wooded area. That dirt road is now paved and called Perry Street. She owned a nice piece of land, about an acre, on which her house stood, along a little dirt lane that ran off Perry St. at that time. The little lane doesn't exist anymore and all the lots where houses stood are thickets now, as though nothing had ever been there. Grommau's lot was rectangular in shape and about half of it was cleared and used as gardening space. She had a sturdy little storage building in her back yard which she, and all of us, called her smoke house. Smoke houses were not used for people to puff on cigars and cigarettes, but for the curing and flavoring of meats. Grommau's smoke house, though, was filled with all kinds of stored up junk, and no meat. Grommau was a maid in the home of one Denson Barnett. I remember seeing her being transported many times to and from home in the back seat of the Barnett's car. In those days colored people had to "ride in the back." I never knew Grommau to be married, nor have children of her own. She raised my mother's two oldest children, after they initially lived with Momma and Daddy for a while on the Lake Bottoms. My mother's two oldest children were from her first marriage. When my siblings and I were little ones, and Momma and Daddy would often be at each other's throats, Momma would head off to Grommau's house dragging us along. My Daddy had difficulty holding in his frustrations about bothersome things. Even though Grommau also made her frustrations known, she was always there for us.

My mother and father married in 1942. They stayed married twenty-some years. In fact, Momma told me she and

Arthur L. "Lump" Ford, 1898 – 1985

Arthur was a son of Milton and Lucrecia Ford. He was a notorious timber man and traveled as a star Lumberjack, constantly winning contests. His tool sharpening ability was unequaled, above master. He sharpened saws for the people of Louisiana and people in parts of Arkansas and Texas. He worked well into his 70s deadening timber and planting trees, and also sharpening saws for the Bossier Parish School Board. (Courtesy of the Arthur Ford family.)

Daddy were married twenty-one years. I felt that was quite an accomplishment despite the finalization of their divorce in 1963. Their marriage was turbulent throughout, but they tried to make it work. It was the second marriage for both. Eventually, they just tended not to listen to each other's explanations or points of view. It was the better times in the midst of all the turmoil that I reflect on and cherish the most. There were many good times, despite Momma and Daddy's eventual breakup, which definitely solidified us as a viable family. Momma and Daddy had seven children together, five girls and two boys.

Perkins Ford, 1902 – 1981, Captain, U.S. Army

Shown here in his 1st Lieutenant uniform, "Uncle Weavie," as we all called him, was very disciplined militarily and otherwise. He is the twelfth child of Milton and Lucrecia Ford. He entered the Army in about 1921, just after WWI, and served over 30 years therein. He was a captain for some years and was said to have been promoted to the rank of Major shortly before retiring in the mid-1950s. (Courtesy of the Arthur Ford family.)

CHAPTER FIVE
Early School Days

It didn't take a Ph.D. for me to figure out why people were was gathering in large numbers on the Lake Bottoms to work those cotton fields. All I had to do was think. A thinking man becomes dangerous in the Brier Patch, you see. Even so, I don't believe most of the people eking out a living in the cotton fields bothered finding the "big picture." As for me, that is where I made my stand, looking at the big picture from the beginning. It seems to me that the first law of nature in a capitalist society is to assess and understand what your economic status is, just as the first law of nature itself is self-preservation. Experience should help you figure this out quickly. You have needs, and you pay to satisfy them. You probably don't need a lesson in economics, but I am here to tell you that where I am from, we worked. Evidently, a lot of hands got forced where we lived. The area wasn't the Mississippi Delta, but it could very well have been called the North Louisiana Delta. Motorized transportation in these areas was a necessity that relatively few people could afford. Therefore, most of us just walked where we needed to go, day or night, whether it was church, visiting, or school. There was a custom in our area in which even some of the white folks participated: People would actually stop their vehicles and give you a ride, as though they already knew where you were going. Many times no words were even spoken. A wave of the hand sometimes sufficed. That is how most people got around.

Not long after we moved back to Bolinger and into our new house, after having sharecropped on the Lake Bottoms,

it was just about time for me to start school. I can't say I was
the most unfortunate person who attended Carrie Martin High
School in Plain Dealing, Louisiana. On the other hand, I can't
say I was the most fortunate, either. Carrie Martin High School
was a twelve-grade school, from first to twelfth. I got off to a
rocky start, a very traumatic experience indeed. My first day of
school ever was like going to the slaughter house. People were
acting all nervous and startled and moving about as though
they were being herded somewhere. So I guess I was the only
one that had the nerve to just go ahead and cry about it. I
hadn't seen so many people in one place, in such close proxim-
ity in my life before. Everybody was walking all over the place,
bumping into everybody else and scaring me with big strange
faces without smiles. I cried so much that day that everybody
knew who the "Ford" boy was—my first mistake. After a
while, I realized that crying wasn't helping my situation at all. It
did nothing but cause laughs. I got separated from Momma so
much that when she found me I had to figure out who she was.
Then she started acting like she didn't want to know who I was.
Of course, by that time I had made friends with some little
rowdy fella, and we were out there running round in circles like
two little laughing fools, falling down. We'd pick ourselves up
off the ground, run around some more, fall down, and laugh
some more. Then, all of a sudden things started looking familiar, and I started wondering why everybody else was walking
around with long faces.

My younger brother and baby sister got the chance to
go to kindergarten school. I remember how everyone thought
it was a great addition to the Plain Dealing Negro community to have a real kindergarten school, a place where children
could learn numbers and alphabets before they even reached
first grade. The well-known woman who operated it was Miss
Annie Mae. That's what everybody called her. She was a short,

Daddy's Little Pride and Joy

Authur "Lump" Ford, with his little pride and joy, my youngest sister Mary. Mary was the baby in our family and could do no wrong. The fence in the background surrounded the house in Bolinger. The gate always stayed open, just as it is in the photo, which didn't really matter, for anything seeking entry could simply climb through the large openings anyway. (Courtesy of the Arthur Ford family.)

heavy set, soft-voiced, pleasant-talking woman who always managed a smile. She and Ernest Burnham operated in an admirable business-like manner in that location, on the northwest corner of Crabapple Ave. and Birch, across from Perry St. Mr. Honess, as we all called him, ran a little refreshment stand on the same premises. This is where the folks would gather to buy and eat flavorful snow cones, especially after being dropped off there by the cotton-chopping and cotton-picking trucks that brought them from the Lake Bottoms. I don't know when Miss Annie Mae's kindergarten school closed, but I do know that it stayed in operation for years, and I remember being proud of her and Mr. Honess.

I had the misfortune of having to start right out in first grade without experiencing the benefit of kindergarten. My birthday had indeed worked against me, my second mistake. I was too early for one year and too late for the other, depending on how you break it down. This was the last year before kindergarten started in our area. I entered first grade when I was five years old. My birthday was January 21st, which put me smack dab in the middle of no man's land, a place where you find yourself always on the hot seat, exposed, going against the grain, and always having to be creative in order to survive. Having to be a maverick isn't easy, my third mistake.

In 1952 I actually started school, even though I was officially acknowledged as a first grader in 1953. So, in September of 1952, I was five years old and in first grade. I earned an A and B report card that first year and got to where I was daring any other student to challenge me. I remember when Miss Harris, my first grade teacher, who later became Miss Lee, told me to not write my letters and numbers so perfect. It was not that I took more than my share of time in class writing them; it was simply the only way I knew how to write them. Even at that young age I already knew the difference between making progress and holding up progress, and I remember that I was the one she selected to help the other students, and that reassured me that I was doing it right and was on the right track. I also remember not knowing how to tell her that was the only way I knew how to write, so I kept up the good work, and, as a result, still pride myself on exceptional legibility. Being gifted with special talents is rare, and being fortunate enough to develop those talents is even rarer. In my case, I always found myself trying to develop my talents regardless of my fortune. In later years, Miss Lee became a loyal follower of my musicianship, guitar playing, and vocal performances. When I was in high school, she often invited me to come and play and sing

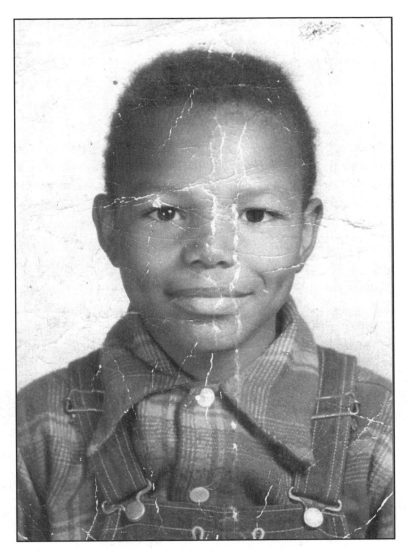

Arthur Lee Ford, Jr.

This photo is of me in first grade. Notice the overalls and flannel shirt. In those days, if your shirt wasn't buttoned at the top you weren't considered a man. (Courtesy of the Arthur Ford family.)

for her classes. I obliged her and was quite honored to do so. Other teachers would come in and watch. I never forgot those times and still feel proud that I was chosen to touch lives that way. Before I reached high school, though, I found myself paying some hefty dues at the hands of Miss Lee and others.

In first grade I remember we didn't have rest rooms in the wooden buildings. In fact, for the duration of my entire school career the frame buildings never had rest rooms. At that time the new elementary school building hadn't been built, and they did not allow us rowdy elementary school children up there in the high school building. In the early days we had to use a big black five-gallon bucket for rest room purposes. Now imagine a first grader having to climb up on a huge bucket, and on top of that, having to balance—and this never changed. Plus, guess where this big black five-gallon bucket was kept— wait, everybody together now—"In the cloakroom!" The cloakroom was where practically everything was kept, such as shoes, coats, mops, brooms, or a dirty pair of pants somebody pooped in. And the window was much too high for us kids to reach it. Our problem was that we were trying to hold it in just to keep from having to go into the cloakroom and face that big old black five-gallon bucket. But facing it was exactly what all of us did, because somebody was always knocking the thing over. And the only nice, polite, cleanup crew available was us—a real circus. I never did get around to asking anybody what a cloak was. All I know is that I was scared to go into the cloakroom because there was a smaller room at the end of it that stayed dark, and maybe that was where the cloak lived and would come out at any time to get me.

In September 1953, on the first day of school, I was sitting near the end of a table in the second grade room, next to the entrance. The noise level was loud from everybody talking and being happy because they were passing on to the second grade. No teacher had come into the room yet, and we were just getting carried away with ourselves, though we remained in our seats. This was in a frame, or wooden building that eventually became the three-classroom seventh grade department, after a new brick building was built to house the lower elementary classrooms. Suddenly, my left peripheral vision caught some movement. I quickly turned my head in that direction and saw Miss Harris appear franticly from the first grade room, her right side to us. I noticed her face had an expression of desperation as she walked hurriedly from the room. After about three paces out of the first grade room she stopped quickly and looked to her right, directly into the second grade room. Her eyes met mine. She quickly relaxed and made a snappy right turn and marched straight to me with hurried steps. When she entered the room everyone got really quiet. She grabbed me by my left arm, pulled me out of my seat, while saying, looking straight ahead and not at me, "Where do you think you're going?" I had no choice but to walk with that woman, "'cause she meant business!" If anything was said after that, I don't know. Needless to say, I was one shocked kid who thought he was going to second grade because he had passed. I was treated by Miss Harris as though I were fully aware that I was under contract to stay in first grade and better not ask any questions and better not breach it. She took me back into that first grade room and offered me absolutely no explanation. That haunted me all through my entire school career. I knew I had passed that first year. My original report card did in fact show all A's and B's. So why was I being forced to do first grade another year? One day, when I was a senior, someone "volunteered" me to tidy up a room adjoining the principal's office. It didn't take me long to realize that was where the school records were stored—the archives, if you will. I figured out how the system was organized and decided to look for my records to clarify what had bothered me all those years. I had long since lost my report cards and wanted to know whether or not my grades for the two years in first grade were recorded the same on the permanent records, reflecting my true performance, which I had kept in mind through the years. I had to have closure after all those years of worry. Bingo, I found it! I could now lay years of undue worry to rest. The second year was straight A's, just as I remembered! So, with that concrete and accurate knowledge of the records, I decided to discuss the matter with Momma. Momma said she asked about it when it happened and was told that I was too young to proceed to second grade. She said they told her since I started at age five I had to go through first grade again. Well, I was simply floored. Despite all the worrying I did, nothing tops how I remembered being so impressed and proud that my Momma had gone to bat for me. My mother didn't have a leg to stand on against the system, but she stood for justice anyway. That was the greatest thing I took away from the whole ordeal.

I remember quickly accepting and adjusting to the new group of first graders. The girls were as rowdy as the boys and we did raise the roof. Sometime during that school year, I think Miss Harris probably eventually regretted bringing me back to her class, even though I never disrespected her or my classmates. My popularity in elementary school was due to things I did that required bravery and talent. I had a huge following in first grade. Recess and lunch periods were quite enjoyable for the students. We loved going outside to play. There was a little thicket of bushes and undergrowth with a few trees scattered in there across from the playground, in back of the school where the first grade and sixth grade buildings were located. We played all kinds of fun games in that thicket. We ran about in that area so much that there were all kinds of little trails and hiding places in there.

For me, elementary school set the stage for years to come of discipline, direction, and purpose. In elementary school, we sang songs of praise to God, of patriotism, of culture, etc, every morning before classes started. We honored our country in other ways, such as reciting the Pledge of Allegiance to its flag. But I tell you, we students lived for recess and lunchtime. We had a subculture, a rhythm within the outdoors routine of activity. Throughout elementary school, and in fact the entire school scene, there were leaders and there were followers. The leaders simply stepped out and took charge, and as long as they showed direction and demonstrated a working agenda, others would acknowledge it and follow their lead. The teachers recognized things like that and went with the flow. Elementary school was a fun time for students, and the teachers were well trained as well as smart, and they maintained that integrity.

The academic side of elementary school was no problem for me because I liked learning things and working with my hands. I always liked reading and thinking about what I read, all the way through sixth grade. That is one reason I became a slow reader, and never learned the art of cramming or faking. And I was aware of the fact that while I was sitting there thinking about what I read, or what the teacher or speaker had said, some others had moved on, so I was faced with having to catch up in my own way. I guess that is why some people are referred to as freight trains and others are called streamlines. Even in those early days, I loved and treasured my ability to work with my hands and get things done.

To me, working with my hands is a tradition. I remember in third grade being turned on to the sight and sounds of the snare drum, and the rest was school musical history. In early fourth grade, I discovered a cute little yellow Spanish guitar in the attic of Grommau's house—with all six strings on

Hilton Maude Ford, 1941-1955

"Sister Maude," as we called her, was the oldest of seven children from Mozel and Arthur Ford and possessed a great talent and feel for music. She loved being called Hilda. (Courtesy of the Arthur Ford family.)

it! I thought I was in heaven. My sister, Maude, was already a member of the high school marching band and, man, was she talented. It was she who taught me the importance of excellence in musical performance. My sister told me to never get on stage "not ready." She told me to play my best and always nail it for the people. She knew I cherished that advice, and she knew that I knew that she meant it. She was so musically talented that she would fill in wherever the band needed help, even as majorette, and sometimes drum major. I'll always remember how she made me laugh when she told me, and quickly demonstrated, how people love to see the majorettes shake their booties. Turned out, she was right.

When I was in elementary school, Henry Patterson and I dominated the marble-playing circuit. I started playing marbles in third grade and just loved it. Everybody, including myself, discovered that I had quick reflexes and excellent skills. In fourth grade, we played marbles religiously and learned the rules of the game. By the fifth grade, I had learned the differences among the types of marbles and steels. I became a pro at reading the ground as well as the minds of my opponents. In fifth and sixth grades, only Henry Patterson rivaled me, and sometimes actually outplayed me. Henry and I always drew big crowds when we played. Besides me, Henry was the only one I knew who was skillful at shooting, or popping, a marble from a swale, or sunken area. I accomplished this by selecting a medium-sized steel, which was slightly smaller than a regular marble, but heavier. I would fire it on a looping trajectory, causing it to drop into the hole or sunken area, hitting the marble slightly in its rear while hitting the ground at the same time. That caused the marble to pop almost straight up out of the swale. Executed with skill and great judgment, this was one of my favorite shots. Henry also displayed good strategic skills inside the ring. He was a worthy opponent. I never bought any marbles and never stole any—I didn't need to and didn't want to. The action was usually where the new marbles were. There was always someone who was ready to gamble, had new marbles, and was hot to trot. Careless players were always losing their marbles inside and outside the ring. In fact, I got started by finding lost marbles. I even lost a few marbles after I started playing, but eventually learned to keep them tucked away. What we called a "steel" was a favorite shooting piece of the better players. It was a metal ball bearing. The ideal one was shiny with no rust or dark spots. Sometimes you were lucky enough to find one, right out in the middle of the playground. It was always finders-keepers. Everyone always played within the rules and was proud and happy to show off their skills, whether they had any or not. If someone didn't have skills, they quickly found out and eventually became a spectator. Nobody ratted on anybody because everybody was too eager to get out there and either play or watch. It was always fun having the girls come out and mingle with the crowds and watch us play. We had unwritten, but to us official, playing rules and methods of elimination. I remember us having three or four, and sometimes more, rings going at the same time. Then the winners of the various rings would compete, and that is when the crowds got big, gathering around and watching the winners play. Henry Patterson gave me pure "D" hell. That boy brought out the best marble playing skills I had. There were a few other decent players, but Henry is the only one who never left my memory, for he is the one that made me put on a clinic for the people. My marble-playing years ended at the end of sixth grade, and then I eventually put them in the drawer of a homemade desk my brother had built. They stayed in that drawer for years, along with a partially used bar of Camay soap that I loved to smell.

I was approaching my teenage years, more involved in music, and had to turn my attention to other demands. Besides,

Arthur Lee Ford, Jr. - 5th Grade

This is my fifth grade photo from Carrie Martin High School in Plain Dealing, Louisiana. I sure thought I was a man — notice that shirt buttoned at the top again. (Courtesy of the Arthur Ford family.)

Mrs. Lucille Layton got my attention with some academic obstacles she was strategically placing in my path. In fact, I credit Miss Layton for preparing me for seventh grade, where Miss Helen Charles, Mr. Windsor, and Miss Pearl Gibson took over. Of all the things I remember while in seventh grade, the event that stands out most was when a white man came to Miss Gibson's classroom one day and lectured to us about how all men were not created equal. He had three students of different heights go stand in front of the class, side by side, and told us it proved what he said. Then he laid onto the subject of Negroes and whites. He insisted that Negroes were not equal to whites. Everyone remained quiet while the man talked loudly, with a red, excited face. I also remember the fact that nobody believed him.

In fifth grade I started participating in fund-raisers. We sold candy, mostly candy bars. I did an excellent job until I discovered their anti-hunger capacities. I was in Miss Stevens' class during most of my candy-selling saga. A po' boy selling candy is just not a good situation. The same thing that happened to the famous Isaac Hayes happened to me, and I haven't yet quit laughing at that one. He told about how he sold candy when he was in school. He said he ate the candy because he was hungry. I laughed something fierce when I read that, because I definitely related to it. Miss Stevens was very nice about the candy-selling, until the morning I showed up without money or candy. When she asked me where the money was, I told her I had let people have the candy on credit. The next day I told her I had forgot to bring the money. I had never before seen a smile leave someone's face quicker than the one that disappeared from Miss Stevens' face that morning after I said that. Everybody in the classroom was looking at me, laughing. I told her I would have the money the next day. Well, needless to say, the teacher wasn't buying my story, but I didn't know how to tell her I was hungry as hell and simply ate the candy. Those Butternut candy bars got the best of me. I don't remember how long it took me to pay for that candy, but I do remember later feeling really silly for disappointing such a wonderful person, as well as letting my classmates down by adversely affecting our fund-raising efforts, and it has served as a life-long lesson for me. I guess that's one reason I had to swallow the fact that, also in fifth grade, someone stole a brand new pair shoes from me. They were swiped right from under my desk, as I sat in it. I had put them underneath the desk at the beginning of class, but at the end of class they were not there. I had gone to school barefoot many days before because I had no shoes, and as soon as Daddy bought me some I let them get stolen. I never gathered up the nerve to tell Daddy somebody stole the shoes, but I guarantee you, I've been making up for it ever since. I did like Steppin' Fetchit did; I pulled the shoes off so I wouldn't wear them out.

To the lower elementary students, the fifth and sixth graders were the big kids. We big kids not only prided ourselves on marble playing and ball playing, we also had to walk around with a lodestone in our pockets to whip out at the right time and stick it on something, in front of somebody we wanted to impress. A lodestone was nothing other than a magnet, and it was an elementary school status symbol among the boys. It is difficult now to understand how a lodestone could have been a status symbol at the time, but it was.

Second, third, and fourth grades were routine for me, but also interesting. Those were the years when I lived for school-closing night. That was when students were given opportunities to showcase their talents. In fact, I loved school-closing nights throughout my entire school career. One of my most memorable school-closing night performances occurred when I was in elementary school and sang along with a re-cording of Harry Belafonte's "Banana Boat Song," with girls dancing on both sides of me in Hula garb. For years after that, the women in the area and in the cotton fields called me the "banana boat boy." I loved the stage, the colorful lights, and the crowd's appreciation. I also loved all the school activities surrounding Halloween, Thanksgiving, and Christmas. These times also gave all the students many more opportunities to showcase their talents. I liked practicing songs and plays. We square danced a lot in elementary school, and I loved it. In sixth grade, Miss Layton was always having us move the desks out of the way so we could have at it. Of course, there was always someone who just didn't get the hang of it, but for me it was fun and pleasure. I loved swinging the girls around, making them smile.

CHAPTER SIX
Family Years In Bollinger

In the mid-to late-1950s, when we lived in Bolinger, Daddy had a drab green 1949 Ford pickup truck. It was suppose to be our transportation, but it turned out to be more of a headache than a mode of conveyance. It was not the fault of the truck so much as it was from lack of maintenance, however. It seemed like it was years that the truck wouldn't start unless we all gathered around it and pushed it. Even that didn't work sometimes. Then we'd get stuck having to push it back up the incline of the lane to the house to try it again. I remember one day we were all tired and frustrated from pushing the truck. Daddy was bound and determined to get that truck started. He then proceeded to do what I thought was a terrible idea in the first place. He hooked the horse up to the truck. I was thinking the truck would start and run over the horse. Momma was inside the truck to control it in case it started. Daddy was yelling and slapping the horse with the lines like someone gone mad. The horse was in one spot stomping and moving around from side to side, going nowhere. We all stood back, watching the action. In those days you didn't talk back to Mother and Father, and you damn sure didn't tell them what to do. But I yelled out one hell of a "statement" to my daddy that day. I told him the horse couldn't pull that truck. Guess I was trying to speak for the horse. Daddy just decided to ignore me and he tried again. I couldn't stand watching that horse try to pull that truck and Daddy acting in such a terrible manner. All of a sudden Daddy unhooked the horse from the truck and without a word marched the horse back to the lot and put him up. I walked over to the truck and looked at the beat up ground with those hoof prints in it. Mental images of that horse's hysterical eyes and the frantic action of his legs bother me to this day. There is a big difference between breaking a horse and breaking a horse's spirit, a lesson I have never forgotten. If nothing else, I took what happened that day as a lesson.

I was just short of ten years old at that time and had started plowing with the horse. I had already been watching Daddy plow for years. He would always plow the garden, cornfield, and the sweet potato patch. I guess that sealed my fate, because not long after, I started plowing, Daddy quit plowing. Daddy did some things when he plowed that I was determined to improve on. For instance, he would tie the ends of the lines together and run them around his waist. That way he wouldn't have to hold them and the plow at the same time. Well, that may not be a bad idea, as long as the horse doesn't spook or get mad at you and take off running. Another thing Daddy did was run the turn plow too deep and tire the horse out far too quickly, and then start fighting with him. That was the last straw with me. When I started plowing, I put my talent where my mind was. It worked. First I looped both lines at the ends, laid the loops on the handles of the plow, simply ran my fingers through the loops, and then held on to the loops and plow handles at the same time. Therefore, nothing was around my waist as a hazard. If for some reason the horse needed to run, he wouldn't have me with him, having possibly broken my back. When I used the turn plow, especially when I broke new ground, I ran it shallower than Daddy did, at the same time maintaining an effective depth. I learned how to work with the horse and not against him. I learned at that early age that consistency of technique and the repetition of its integrity was an effective method of teaching a horse. I learned how to work the land by watching what my Daddy did. Buddy, the horse, and I got to where we were like two champions at working the land year after year, and I owe it all to Daddy and Grampa.

Every year we had a routine. We planted our garden, cornfield, and sweet potato patch. Sometimes near the east side of the house at the edge of the cornfield, we would plant extra things in a few rows. For instance, one year we would plant Irish potatoes; rural Southerners called them "ice potatoes." The next year we might plant peanuts. Every year Daddy would buy one big bag of commercial fertilizer. We had to make do with that one bag. We spread it by hand and I learned how to spread it to make it last for all the ground we worked. I got to looking forward to that one big bag of fertilizer every year because to me it meant progress. It meant we would get a chance to eat again for another year and Momma could can some food for the winter. It also meant that O'Buddy, as we also called the horse, would once again get that one big bag of grain that Daddy would buy for him once a year. O'Buddy had to pull the plows, so his diet was supplemented with the grain. That special supplement mixture was called "all grain." I loved smelling that mixture of molasses and grains. It was a big burlap bag of grain, half of which was fed to the horse during spring plowing and the other half fed to him during fall harvest plowing. Otherwise, O'Buddy would be turned out to eat grass.

We had an acre and a half or so of woods on our property, with some hills and gullies in them. When I was a little fella I would ride my broom horse through them. Of course, if Momma had realized how the straws were disappearing out of that broom, she would have made me find every one of them and then bring a "poly peach tree" switch to her immediately afterwards, for disciplinary purposes. My brother and some neighbor boys and I played lots of games in those woods. We dug a big hole in the side of an embankment on our property in the woods out near the road that ran along our property frontage. That big hole was our fort. We named it Fort Forooha. That stood for Ford, Root and Haskin, honoring some of our neighboring playmates. I think Daddy would have paddled a few behinds if he knew his land was being shared with the neighbors and the Army. We were a bunch of little guys running around in those woods, and we could easily have gotten bit by some poisonous snakes.

The sights and sounds of the Southern woods are quite distinctive and could serve as a lesson on ecosystems. One thing that really fascinated me was the sight and sound of a group of frantic birds. Normally they would just fly here and there, to and from, mainly hunting for food for themselves and their young offspring. But I observed that birds have a way of sounding an alarm when something out of the ordinary is happening, or present, on the forest floor. They would gather or group in a tree and be very noisy, thus marking the spot where the action was. If they moved constantly from tree to tree it meant that their object of interest was moving. I then knew that if I wanted to see what it was I had to get there, because it would soon leave or travel from the area. I always advanced toward the noisy birds with caution. As I approached the group of birds, I would get within thirty feet of them and imagine a straight, vertical line going from the top of the group of birds in the center, down to the ground. That is where I almost always found what I was looking for. If it weren't at the center point, I would quickly scan a horizontal area on the ground, ten to twenty feet from the center of the group in any direction and would find the object of interest. The object of interest would just about always be a snake. Sometimes the birds would have found some nocturnal creature, or maybe an underground creature, that would be temporarily out of its element. Snakes could grow big and long. Black snakes grew big and long and climbed trees very well. Blue racers could scare—and run—the pants off you if they chased you far enough. I remember us kids getting chased from the mill pond more than once by blue racers. I guess even they knew we should have been at home.

There were three large ponds just west of our house, which we called the "Mill Ponds." When we lived in Bolinger all the ponds had lots of water and teemed with fish, snakes, crawfish, turtles (coodahs, as we called them), frogs, and even leaches, just to name some of the inhabitants. When the plentiful rains came, the ponds would sometimes flood, especially the one near our property. Every so many years that pond would rise so high with flood waters that it would run from the pond and behind the neighboring houses like the Colorado River. It was just west of our property and right behind Sis Pearlie's property, Miss Doll Baby (Willie Mae) and Dan Hudson's property, and Miss Honey's (Alberta Haskin) property. This pond had so many perch and catfish that we never bothered fishing much in the others. The pond that got little or no human activity was the middle pond, because of its lack of accessibility. It wasn't much more than a water-filled marsh surrounded by lots of bushes and weeds. In the late 1800s and early part of the 1900s, this area, including the front portion of our property some years before Momma and Daddy purchased it, was traversed by a scenic horse-and-buggy trail. In our day, long flat-topped banks hugged the ponds, enabling us to see right down onto the waters. The banks were shaded by trees and supported nice, wide, well-traveled foot trails. By this time the old horse-and-buggy road had all but vanished. There were residents on all sides of the ponds. The most frequently visited, for beach-like activities, was the one farthest west of us, near where the old saw mill was once located. The saw mill ceased activity and left only a huge concrete structure. It had big concrete pillars that supported a big, wide, flat concrete roof. As a youngster I often played under the structure. It had a dirt floor and no substantial walls. I found out from Daddy that it had been built to house the mules used at the mill. The pond next to that structure had consistently muddy water, yet hosted much swimming and mud crawling. Mud crawling was a term used to make fun of people in the water who couldn't swim. We shared the water with an abundance of water moccasins swimming along the banks and throughout the entire eastern half of the pond. If a snake were after you, you swam. If you were having fun, you mud crawled. In the late part of the summer the ponds would diminish greatly in water capacity. The pond closest to our property was consistently drying up to a fishing hole, or seining hole, as we called it. When this happened, the deepest part of the pond would host the remaining water and its inhabitants would be concentrated there. This is when we applied a fishing method we called seining. We would take four or five or more burlap bags, called croaker sacks, and undo the side seams all the way down to the bottom, leaving the bottom seam intact. The bag would then be opened out to a long rectangular piece of cloth. The opened bags would be sewn together end-to-end, forming something much like a tennis net. We would sometimes make a seining net thirty or forty feet long. The strongest people would be on each end and in the middle. When all the people were distributed along the net, we then set up, positioning ourselves along the bank, facing the deepest part of the fishing hole. Everyone held on to and supported his or her part of the net. We would then proceed with caution, making sure the bottom of the net maintained contact with the mud at the bottom of the water and at the same time holding up the top part. The people on the ends would lead the way while the middle lagged a bit behind. This shaped the net in a semi-circular or banana-like shape, which helped prevent fish from escaping to the side. With the net in place we would methodically and unhurriedly seine all the way across the fishing hole, maintaining proper form until everyone was out of the water and on the bank. To me this was fun. I did not look at it as work, even though some people fed themselves almost exclusively on fish. We would have buckets with pond water in them setting on the bank to quickly put fish into after finishing a pass with the seine. Many times a single pass would suffice. The fish would be jumping, snakes would be scrambling, crawfish would be chasing you, and the leaches would be around your ankles, feeding like crazy, causing blood to run down. It may not have been completely devoid of hard work, but it sure was fun, and where there is a will there is a way.

One thing you learned early on in life in the rural South was to look for snakes and spiders. With the three mill ponds near our house and with cornfields in the area, snakes were plentiful. They loved eating mice and baby chickens, which loved eating grain. There were poisonous snakes in the woods among the pine trees. They were mostly timber rattlers. Now and then, news would spread that a pulpwood or logging worker had met his death at the fangs of a timber rattler. Water moccasins, also known as cottonmouth moccasins, were numerous around rivers, ponds, and swamps. They could lay you out as quickly as a rattle snake. Black widow spiders were plentiful under and around our house. I use to play with them all the time and never knew of the danger in those days. I was fascinated by the spider's black body and strangely-shaped red spot on its bottom side. I would flip them over and look at that strange red spot.

Our house set high on cement blocks. My brother and I use to play under the house. We had two play plantations under there. One was his and the other was mine. We had little roads going from one to the other. We spent lots of time making things. We made our toys. I once made a wooden toy farm tractor. It was in the shape of a Farmall "H." I made it so the wheels up front could turn, just like the real thing. I took it to school one day to show it to a fellow who had asked me to bring it so he could see it. People gathered around that toy like it was one of today's space shuttles. Everyone was so fascinated by it that I agreed to leave it at school on display for several weeks. I finally told the teacher my crops were getting behind and that I needed it. Guess if you're gonna be a little fella with a play plantation, it'll be just like a real plantation— the crops get behind. She laughed like crazy and then told me to go ahead and take it. Of course, I didn't think what I said was funny until I thought about it years later. I realized I hadn't fooled the teacher at all about any crops, but at least I got my tractor back. Creating images of things in my mind, or looking at something I liked and then constructing it, was serious business with me. I learned how to use the tools Daddy had at home. It wasn't necessarily a big hit with Daddy, but I had things to make. For instance, I was really fascinated by how farm machinery worked. Sometimes when we were working cotton fields near Wardview on the Lake Bottoms, some of us would go over to the cotton gin and rest under the sheds and ports where cotton wagons and tractors were parked. I missed many a snooze lying underneath a wagon studying how it was built and how the wheels turned. I remember making a toy cotton wagon and pulling it with the toy tractor I made. That kind of stuff was so much fun.

By the time I was in the sixth and seventh grades, I was making all kinds of things to play with. I was good at making bows and arrows and flippers (sling shots). To make a bow I would go into the woods looking for a certain young, elastic tree. Pine wasn't suitable. I never did know the name of that ideal tree; all I knew was when I found it that was it. In retrospect, I believe it was a young, four or five foot sweet gum tree.

Sometimes I just cut a branch from a mature sweet gum tree to use as a bow. That thing would bend a long way without breaking. The strength of the bow depended on the diameter and length of the stem of the young tree. If you got one too big, it would put too much tension on your string and maybe break it. Plus, it would be too heavy to carry. Sometimes I would get a larger one and whittle it down to the size I wanted. Once I had sized the proper piece of material for my bow, I notched, or grooved, the ends of it, about an inch up the shaft. The string stayed in place by being tied in the notches. With a homemade bow like this, the strength and tension of the string is what kept the bow bent. I remember getting really lucky once because I found some strong twine. It was the wound kind. I went into the woods and found the right stick, and the rest was all fun. My arrows were made of a weed that grew about four feet or so in height at maturity, and then I would use it when it was dead and dried, causing it to be stiff and tough. I loved watching the trajectory of the arrows as they swished toward the target.

The flipper was my favorite. It was a real stinger that required excellent hand-eye coordination, the right technique, and most of all, superior judgment to operate effectively. To make a flipper all you need is a piece of leather, a strip of rubber and some strong twine. Attach these items properly and you have yourself a choice weapon. For the leather I would find an old shoe or boot that had been abandoned, for I was after the tongue. Once I found a thin, pliable leather tongue, I would cut a rectangular piece about one inch by three inches, put a small hole in each end of the leather strip in the middle, get a four to five inch piece of wound twine, and tie each end in the holes. I would get an old bicycle inner tube which is thin, easily stretched, and recoils just fine and dandy, and cut a strip of rubber from it about a half inch wide and fifteen to twenty inches long. As a matter of preference I would cut my strip from either the extreme upper portion of the inner tube or the extreme inner portion of the inner tube. In my opinion, a strip from those areas would stretch true to form. For instance, if you cut your strip from the side wall of the inner tube, it may tend to curve with the wall. But no matter where you cut it from, that stretched rubber strip should send a small projectile on its way nicely. After you have cut your rubber strip, you simply tie one end of it in a hard knot to the middle of the twine. I used small stones for ammunition. I shot cans, sticks, and bottles. I even shot through open doors of outhouses. But when I shot a bird out of a tree once, I felt so bad that I retired my flipper.

Even though Daddy brought neither government welfare nor much money into the house, he was much more productive than my Momma was giving him credit for being. Daddy only had a second-grade education, but economic necessity made him develop some pretty good survival skills. He told me how he had once worked at Ford Motor Company in Richmond, California, and sent money back home to Momma to save for our new house to be built in Bolinger. In those days, there was what seemed like fake food subsidies available to poor folks, called commodities. The old folks always threw me for a loop when they referred to the food subsidies as "mod-dessy." Now and then I would hear someone ask Daddy if he was going to go get some "moddessies." I remember Daddy bringing something home once that appeared to be processed cheese and powdered milk. They tasted so terrible that we left them on a shelf over the kitchen counter for months on end, and even the mice didn't eat them. The powdered milk had become a solid substance, and the cheese, still in its original box, had lost all its moisture. It was me who eventually threw that stuff away, and that was it.

I always valued Momma and Daddy's efforts to raise and protect their children. It wasn't difficult for me to see the great odds against which they fought. I remember when Daddy hauled pulpwood. Before that, he worked in logging, before my time. Sometimes the physical stress and strain of that work killed men. For instance, that was when pulpwood was loaded by hand, even during my time. If it didn't kill you, it made a he-man of you. It was very common in the South to see men, especially colored men, looking like great athletes. It wasn't from spending time in a gym, but from working hard to survive.

Daddy was a champion lumber jack. He would travel to various parts of the South winning what they called "contests." At the contests they would do things like cut big logs in two with an axe, or saw, to see who could finish first. What captured my attention most was when Daddy told me how he and Woodrow Rance, his partner, would beat the chain saws through logs with a crosscut saw, and he said Woodrow fainted almost every time they did that. I knew Daddy was quite accurate. Not only did he display a sawing technique that I never saw anyone equal or outperform, but he was a superb saw sharpener, better than master. I am proud to say that I learned from a champ, my father. When my Daddy and I would fell a tree and cut off the branches, I couldn't wait to get to the sawing part. We would saw the tree up in blocks and split the blocks into stove-size wood with the axe. For years, we had a wood-burning stove in the kitchen for cooking and a wood-burning heater in the front room. Daddy demonstrated perfect sawing technique, from which I learned the importance of proper rhythm in sawing. He told me to always finish the stroke, and always allow your partner to finish his stroke. This is accomplished most efficiently by both parties positioning themselves properly at the saw and allowing for a full, free-flowing motion of the arms. Pull the saw straight across the log, and keep it oiled. Whether hand-sawing, buck-sawing, crosscut-sawing, or other, keep the saw oiled. Oiling of a saw and proper sawing technique help the teeth of a saw do their job. Daddy and I had sawdust flying like rooster tails out of those logs. One regret I have is that I never got to see Daddy and Woodrow in action together. Daddy had a way of dispensing oil onto a saw that I never saw before or since. Before we left the house for the woods, Daddy would get an empty Coca-Cola bottle and fill it about three quarters full with coal oil. When we got to the job site he would gather a handful of green pine needles, bunch them together, and force them into the mouth of the bottle, leaving about three or four inches sticking out. He would then lay the needles across the trunk of a tree, take the axe and cut off the needles, leaving about two inches sticking out of the bottle. Those needles would be tightly packed in the mouth of that bottle like a cork in a wine bottle, thus resulting in a perfect oil dispenser. Tilting the saw with one hand and employing a whipping motion to the bottom half of the saw with the bottle in the other hand, he would apply a coating of oil without spilling or wasting it.

Contests were often covered by the news media. Daddy was not allowed to kiss the contest queen because she would be a white woman, and he was not considered a white man. Daddy once told me that he went to win the contest, not to kiss the white woman. I remember always wishing that he could have somehow gotten that point across to the white people; perhaps he did. Momma and Daddy never said things to us children that degraded other people—nobody. That is something I value to this day.

People, colored and white, from all over Bossier and some other parishes brought their saws of all types to our house for my Daddy to sharpen. I sometimes laughed when Daddy talked about how some people tried to sharpen their own saws,

Crosscut Saw

This two-person saw was used to cut wood by the Arthur Ford family of Bossier Parish for many years. (Courtesy of the Arthur Ford family.)

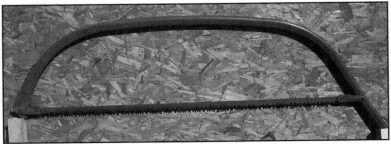

Buck Saw

This saw was used by the Arthur Ford family of Bossier Parish to cut wood for cooking and heating. (Courtesy of the Arthur Ford family.)

or had someone else try to sharpen them. One day I decided to look at what he was talking about. Some of the saws had the teeth rounded from someone's terrible filing, or someone had filed some teeth down much shorter than others. What gets me is Daddy never charged extra for correcting all that abusive stuff. To bring a saw back from that kind of abuse takes one highly skilled master at his craft. I would look at saws when Daddy finished them. No matter what saw Daddy sharpened or corrected, he left the entire row of teeth awesomely symmetrical. I was just astounded at Daddy's ability to file, or cut, those teeth so straight and proper, each and every one, with an amazing precision and consistency, or "sameness." Daddy was unequaled at that, and he knew it. He showed me his instruction book on how to sharpen saws. He even let me prepare a saw for sharpening once. The tools used to sharpen saws were not all that complicated, but were very interesting and effective in their functions. The two basic tools were called the setter and the gauge. There were various files of different types and lengths adapted to whatever saw sharpening job Daddy was going to do. Most of the files Daddy bought were eight inches in length because that size was most suitable to his filing chores. One of my favorite files was the triangular file. This was a small multi-purpose file with three cutting sides. Each side was of a different coarseness. Daddy used the triangular file with great precision on hand saws, for instance. Another interesting little file was round, and quite useful. It was called a rat-tail file. It was shaped like the tail of a rat and was adapted to touch-up situations and corrective work in areas unsuitable for flat or triangular files. Let's say there was a nick or nasty little abrasion at the base of a drag tooth on a crosscut saw or a bucksaw. These teeth, being rounded at the base on both sides, are more easily accessed by a rat tail file than a flat-faced or a triangular file. In other words, a round file can more effectively be used to return the rounded area to its original form. The setter was a tool much like an athletic hand grip developer. There were different setter designs. And for setting the huge cutting teeth of a crosscut saw, Daddy sometimes used a thick, five-inch-long metal piece with an expanded head-like area on one end, against which the tooth would be forced into proper position with a narrow-headed hammer. A setter had two spring-loaded handles that activated a pin inside a grooved head attached to the top of the handles. The action of the pin forced a tooth outward into its proper position, thus "setting" it. You would start at the left end of the saw, or saw blade, and set all the cutting teeth, or cutters, facing you in consecutive order. After completing that side you will turn the saw around and work the other side in the same manner. The gauge tool is simply used to top-dress and side-dress the teeth. Gauging, or dressing the teeth, is another interesting and necessary procedure if you are to turn out a properly sharpened saw. The gauge is a tool about three by six inches in size and about three fourths of an inch deep. It has two deep horizontal groves at the top. These grooves are cut into an "overhang" atop the gauge. In the groove, you will place a flat file about eight inches in length. The file is held in position by small set screws. The file acts to even out, or deburr, the teeth.

You would be amazed at how saw teeth can become jagged and uneven when dulled. When saw teeth become dull they are smooth and shiny on the tips and edges. The cutters become upright in position, thereby inhibiting the performance of the drag teeth. Drag teeth, or drags, must drag or take out the sawdust or shavings. If the teeth don't function properly, a saw will hang up, or jam in the wood and cease to cut at all. That is why teeth have to be set and gauged. So the gauging tool is moved lightly along the top of the saw's teeth. During this procedure you can actually feel the file doing its job. Sometimes the file is actually stopped by a tooth that is slightly longer than others, which is a good example of why the teeth need to be gauged, or dressed, in the first place.

Usually there are several teeth of irregular length along the saw, pitched at ever so slightly different degrees. Therefore, you must gently move the gauge back and forth, letting the file cut the extra points. This makes all the teeth even—the same length or height. Once you achieve a continuous, nonstop motion from one end of the saw to the other, you have a properly gauged saw. In fact, it is this "sameness" of saw tooth length that must be maintained and protected during sharpening. For instance, if you file too much on one tooth it becomes shorter than the others, thereby ruining the sharpening job. There is no margin for error because a saw with jagged teeth simply does not work properly. This is just one reason my Daddy was more than a master at his craft. Untalented people don't understand this type of detail and don't rise to this level of professionalism. They ruin their saws and tools and don't understand why. This is where Daddy stood out. He had eagle eyes and sturdy hands, maintaining symmetry throughout the job.

It is now time to gauge, or dress, the sides of the teeth in a manner similar to top-dressing the teeth. The only difference is you put the file in the vertical groove on the gauge. When you are done setting and gauging a saw it is now ready for sharpening. This is what "separated the men from the boys" and the pros from the amateurs. Daddy was a master technician, worthy of emulation. Daddy sharpened saws for the public for years and never kept a written record of who

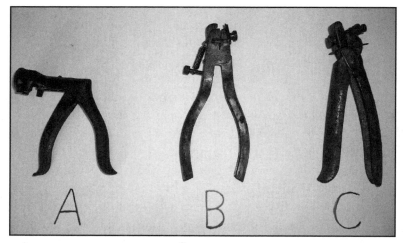

Setters

These saw sharpening tools were owned and used by my dad, Arthur Ford, Sr., of Bossier Parish, Louisiana. They are three different types of teeth setters. Setter A, for instance, was most suited to setting Buck Saw teeth. (Courtesy of the Arthur Ford family.)

owed him what, nor how many saws he sharpened over the years. When he finished sharpening a saw, he would set it under the window on the west end of the front porch. There was always a group of saws under that window, and none of us children were allowed to handle them. They waited there, only to be picked up by their owners. Many times people came to the house when Daddy wasn't there, and they picked up their saw. They would always say, "Tell Lump I'll be back to pay him." I don't remember anyone ever leaving money with us for the services Daddy provided. I do remember that when Daddy got home and we told him someone came and picked up a saw, he would check through the saws to determine who had come and got their saw. He would always know, and would mention names. Daddy kept all that stuff in his head. He was well known in the "Arklatex" area in several professions, especially the timber industry.

When Daddy worked in logging and pulpwood he knew how to rate and classify trees and lumber. In his seventies he still sharpened saws for the Bossier Parish School Board. He was also in his seventies when he headed a timber-deadening and tree-planting crew. Woodrow Rance, Daddy's contest partner, was a white man who had a radio and television repair and rental business, from which Daddy got a television set that required the insertion of a quarter into a slot so that it could play. If you dropped a quarter into the slot, it would play for three hours, the quickest three hours I ever saw go by. Well, my sister Hazel found a slug somewhere and put it in the slot. The television actually played. About three months later, Woodrow came to the house all happy and laughing, talking to Daddy. Before he left the house, he had loaded the television set onto his truck and stomped his hat into the ground. I think Daddy lost his contest partner over that deal.

Daddy would often send my brother and me to the

woods to cut, split, and transport firewood. Now, my brother and I brought back more arguments to the house than wood. Besides, we weren't too crazy about bringing back a lot of wood, because our sisters used the wood for heating metal hair-straightening combs much more than for cooking. They would make a fire in the stove, pull up a chair, and change the kitchen into a beauty shop. Straightening their hair was serious business with my sisters. Daddy said they were cooking brains. Of course, though, when it came to cooking food, the girls didn't and wouldn't make fires. It was an unwritten code that they just didn't know how. They always let us "men folks" know that it was our job to make fires. After I made the fire, as almost always, the arguing would start as to who was going to cook. Sometimes the little wood we had brought to the house burned out before a decision was reached. My sister Maude was usually told to cook. Well, Maude had to follow a ritual every time, and nobody was going to change it. She started out by sweeping the floor and leaning on the broom a lot, daydreaming. It was customary for all of us to take turns easing through the kitchen and out the back door just to see if she had started yet. Maude rivaled Momma and Daddy at making biscuits, but there were nine of us and Maude would almost always bake one skillet of seven biscuits, seldom more. The biscuits were so good that Maude would always eat one or two of them before she would call the rest of us. It took Maude hours to do what she did, but we were all happy just to get a taste.

One of my favorite times of the year was when we gathered ripe vegetables from the garden. We raised peas, beans, tomatoes, squash, hot peppers, onions, turnip greens, mustard greens, and other vegetables. In the South, the growing season is long because of the warm climate. Sometimes we would plant two crops in the same year in the same location. For instance, mustard greens grew fast and were quick to mature. We planted them in sections called beds, even though they can also be planted in rows. Beds of greens yielded more because there would be no wasted space. A bed of greens would measure about six by ten feet. Under good conditions, you can plant two and three stands of greens a year in the same bed. After you use up the first stand of greens you must immediately cultivate the bed with nothing more than a stiff pronged garden rake, fertilize it, if necessary, and then just spread the seeds. The seeds of these types of greens are so small that you do not need to cover them with dirt. If you are lucky enough to plant the greens just before a nice rain, or maybe you water them yourself, the process will be expedited. Turnip and collard greens take a little longer, produce differently, and are more effective when planted in rows, like cabbage greens.

In the Southern woods, there grew something Negroes called poke salad. Momma knew how to cook poke salad, and she cooked it as much as she cooked anything else. Poke salad is not what it sounds like. You do not eat it in a salad as a leafy vegetable. I don't remember eating salads in those days anyway. Poke salad is a tall weed with big, wide, dark green leaves that grows wild in the woods. It was very much a part of poor folks' food chain. I never knew of anyone growing poke salad in their garden, for it was notoriously poisonous. If you eat poke salad right off the stalk you should have your grave already dug so that you can just fall in. And if you don't know how to cook it properly, don't cover up that grave yet. Cooked properly, poke salad has a palatable taste almost like spinach and also like my favorite, mustard greens. Poke salad is like chittlins or certain mushrooms—prepared wrong, it could kill you; prepared properly, it helps you live.

In the early years, Momma would cook and can food from the garden and cornfield at home. Most of the produce from our cornfield and garden were used for canning.

Momma would can some of the tastiest soup. She canned in quart and half-quart Mason jars. This chore took some smart managing. First of all, the ingredients needed to ripen around the same time, which was determined, or controlled, by the planting schedule. In the later years, she would go to the canning house in Plain Dealing. I loved the warm, breezy summer days when Momma would sit on the front porch near the main doorway and prepare peas and beans for cooking. She would usually have us help her. We would shell and snap peas and beans. Each one of us would have a bowl to shell and snap in. When we finished shelling the few peas or beans we had in our bowls, we children would then walk over to Momma and pour the contents into Momma's big bowl. To see that big bowl of shelled and snapped peas and beans setting in Momma's lap and seeing her hands shell and snap those peas and beans was just a blessing to me. The smell of freshly picked peas or beans cooking with some dry-salt meat and onions made me feel like I was living in God's house. Crowder peas are my all-time favorite, fresh or dried. And I just loved it when Momma cooked fried field corn. We only grew field corn. We didn't grow popcorn, and I, for one, didn't know about sweet corn in those days. If you catch field corn at its peak stage of ripeness you can experience some good eating. You can prepare field corn in various ways. For instance, you could boil it on the cob, cook it in soup or gumbo, fry it, etc. The way Momma fried that corn in a skillet made me just want to dive over into it and not come out until it was all gone.

Every winter, when we ran out of canned food, the last thing we had left was cha-cha. Momma always canned some of it every year. Cha-cha to me was like a last-resort, fill-in food, a real non-food food item whose taste was tolerable only when everything else in the food department was absolutely gone. And strangely enough the main use for cha-cha as a food was to enhance the taste of other foodstuffs, like a type of relish. Daddy was the only one I knew who would eat cha-cha like it had won a blue ribbon at the local county (parish) fair. To the best of my knowledge cha-cha was made from finely chopped cabbage greens, heavily spiced, and left alone for a few weeks in a tightly sealed jar with pickling sauce and water until it was ready for consumption.

During the spring and summer months, Sis Pearlie would give us milk and butter. She had about an acre and a half of land, a nice little rectangular strip, on which she also kept a very productive milk cow. I never could figure out how that woman was so efficient with one cow and did the same thing, year after year, after year. Her name was Pearlie Mae McDonald, but we all just called her Sis Pearlie. She was a neat,

Plow – Cultivator

This plow was owned and used by the Arthur Ford family of Bossier Parish, Louisiana. It is a horse-drawn plow and was used for soil aeration and weed control. (Courtesy of the Arthur Ford family.)

clean person with a pretty little house and yard to match. Her house and yard were fenced in, on her total property which was fenced in. Inside her yard she grew all kinds of pretty flowers, roses and lilacs, among other things. She had some big bushes growing that produced colorful flowers shaped like the long bell of a trumpet, which attracted beautiful, colorful hummingbirds. Her yard was simply gorgeous and gave off the most attractive fragrances. Sis Pearlie cooked lots of cakes and pies and would always share them with our family. Her family didn't live around Bolinger, but Clyde Murry's son, Walter, who lived out of state, was related to her somehow, as well as to my Daddy. Clyde Murry lived along the Dogwood Drive, now Ford Road, and was married to my Daddy's cousin Mary before she passed away. He kept a picture of Aunt Mary on his piano. She was a beautiful woman. It was her family of Fords, Daddy told me, who inherited the twelve hundred acres of land from a plantation owner in the Plain Dealing area, including a huge portion of the Lake Bottoms. Sis Pearlie also had a son, Buster, who visited her once a year.

I figured out later that Sis Pearlie knew we struggled to keep food on the table, so she just simply helped us. Whenever we would hear her holler "Uh, Sus Mo," from her screened in back porch we knew she had some food to give us, or she needed help with something. She would specify which. "Sus Mo" was what Sis Pearlie called Momma. Sis Pearlie was a sickly woman, and we would all respond to her alarms. She would have fainting spells and fits. An epileptic seizure was known in the South as a "fit." So at some point every day we would check on Sis Pearlie. When Daddy checked on Sis Pearlie he also checked in her refrigerator. Daddy was always saying how Sis Pearlie had "sody waters in her 'frigerator." He said she had no business drinking them, because they were not good for her. He would then always go on to say how he should drink the sody waters just to keep her from drinking them. When Sis Pearlie milked her cow, she would do her churning on her back porch. When I would hear that galuking sound coming from over there, I knew I would soon be "volunteered" to go and get the milk and butter. One time we were on our front porch shelling peas and beans. Sis Pearlie yelled out the call, and Momma yelled back to her, acknowledging it. Sure enough, Momma said, "June, go get the milk and butter." Now, all of us there, and she picked me. I was so mad, and all my siblings were laughing. When I came back to the house, I still had a few of those big crocodile tears dropping from my eyes. I walked right past everybody, including Momma, who was in her regular position, blocking half the front doorway, on my way to the refrigerator. Just before I got to the refrigerator Momma spoke out and said, "Bring cher, June." I looked around, with wet

Turn Plow

This right-action horse-drawn turn plow was owned and used by the Arthur Ford family of Bossier Parish, Louisiana. It is a multi-purpose plow appreciated mostly for its ability to break new ground. (Courtesy of the Arthur Ford family.)

eyes, still holding the milk and butter, and blurted out, "What chair!?" When all of them let out a loud group laugh I then realized what Momma was saying. I immediately stopped crying and started laughing. What she meant was "Bring it here, June." My sister Maude teased me about that ever after. But from that time on I always laughed to myself with pride and appreciation while going to get the milk and butter from Sis Pearlie, because it took that situation to make me understand that not only did getting mad make no sense but, I realized that she was simply helping us.

The soils in our cornfield, sweet potato patch, and the garden were all different but highly suitable for growing food. Even though most Bolinger residents had good soil around their houses, the remainder of the Bolinger area was plentiful in red clay and pine trees. Southern red clay is sticky and heavy when wet. It is generally not suitable for growing food, but, at the same time, its productivity is highly dependent on one's need or desire to work it for growing food. We had a relatively big garden area that was just ideal for growing food. The soil was a dark sandy-loam. Drainage was good and weeding wasn't a burdensome chore. The garden was weeded by hoeing, or chopping, much like chopping cotton. Once we did the initial weeding for the season, Daddy or I would control the weeds for the rest of the growing season through cultivation by plowing with the horse. The sweet potato patch was quite a large area, too. It adjoined the east side of Sis Pearlie's property. Every year Daddy would buy sweet potato slips, or plants, that came in bundles. The slips were about eight to ten inches in length. The whole family would participate in planting the sweet potato slips because of the various phases, or divisions, of labor required. Daddy, in the early years, and I, in the later years, would have already prepared the ground. This was done with the turn plow and the middle buster. We never had the luxury of owning a disk, so we used garden rakes for breaking up and pulverizing the soil for planting. We didn't break up the entire plowed area with the rakes, just the rows or furrows we intended to plant. We had worked the soil so many years that the ground was quite manageable, otherwise a disk would have been mandatory. Once we turned the soil of the sweet potato patch, it was loose enough to bust a middle, or furrow. This furrow would be deep, leaving a levee-like row, forming a row-furrow pattern for the entire planting area. We used the biggest and widest sweep we had on the middle buster plow for clearing the sweet potato patch rows, or furrows at this point. This was because of the relatively large size of a mature sweet potato. It is in this big furrow where the sweet potato slips would be planted, or "set out." Before the slips were set out in the furrow, the furrow had to be prepared in a special way. First of all, we fertilized it, and then we had to get some dirt back into the furrow so we would have a base in which to set out the slips. To accomplish this, we would again hook the horse to the turn plow and go along the right side of the left row, the mound or levee-like part, peeling off just a little bit of dirt back into the middle. When we reached the end of the row, we would turn the horse around and go back up the same middle, peeling of a little bit of dirt from the right side of the row to the left. When we got to the end of the row and looked back, we would see a little row down in between the two big rows. The little row is where the potato slips were planted, and watered at the time of planting. The big rows were left alone at this time, for their purpose would be served later. If for some reason someone didn't make a little row with a turn plow they could take a cultivator plow, which has a two-sweep setup, make one pass between the two big rows and create a little row in the middle, even though this method would be of a lesser quality than with the turn plow. The least desirable method was taking a garden rake and by hand making a little row in the middle. So, following the turn plow method will reveal the entire patch as little rows between big rows.

When I would finish plowing and preparing the ground for planting, I would take the harness off the horse and put him up. I would then go back and help set out slips. We planted sweet potato slips twelve to fifteen inches apart so that each plant could produce its maximum yield without competition from its neighboring plant, or even the weeds. Twelve to fifteen inches apart also allowed ample room to accommodate a hoe during weeding, because we didn't want to cut down any of

Middle Buster

This horse-drawn plow was owned and used by the Arthur Ford family of Bossier Parish, Louisiana. You may not find this name in Webster's dictionary but any hard working country boy can tell you all about it. This multi-purpose plow was used for unearthing underground produce such as turnips, potatoes, or peanuts, etc., and establishing plowed ground with rows and middles for planting purposes. (Courtesy of the Arthur Ford family.)

the potato plants. Sweet potato slips grow, spread, and mature to become vines running along the ground. The potato itself grows on the plant underground. Each surviving plant usually produces several potatoes. The potatoes do not always mature to the same size. Some are suited to baking whole and others, the very large ones, are more suited to making pies or yams. We would usually run out of potatoes before the worst part of winter and would go back out in the patch and scrounge, or "root," using a shovel, hoe, or a long-pronged garden rake, for small or even underdeveloped ones that we might have previously rejected or just didn't uncover during the harvest. Sometimes we would even dig again later, with greater desperation, using a shovel or a long-pronged garden rake; occasionally, we were pleasantly surprised. Momma made some of her tastiest meals from such irregular harvests. Sweet potatoes were stored by most people in a dry place, in a dirt-filled container of some sort, usually a huge, lidded, wooden box. Some people would just leave their potatoes in the ground for storage and dig only those ones they wanted to eat at that particular time. If someone did that, they didn't plant many, because potatoes will rot quickly if neglected for long, especially when left outside underground in an overly moist environment.

After the young sweet potato plants grow several inches taller, before starting to spread, or vine, is when the big levee-like dirt row becomes involved in the process. The objective now is to provide cover, or ground, for the actual potato to grow in. Perhaps four to maybe six weeks have passed since the slips were first planted and they have now grown and strengthened. Time to harness the horse and get the trace hooked up to that singletree dangling on the end of the old turn plow, for it is time to throw some more dirt. With the turn plow I threw half of the dirt row up around one side of the row of potatoes and half of the other dirt row up around the same row of potatoes by coming back down the same middle. A turn plow, by the way, is the heaviest-duty among the various plows available. A single-edged turn plow throws dirt only one way, either to the right or to the left. Our turn plow threw the dirt to the right. A double-edged turn plow throws dirt both ways. Any ground can be worked with a turn plow, and it is ideal for breaking new ground because of the strong, sturdy, durable construction of its moldboard. The moldboard is the metal part that goes into the ground. It is an assembly of several parts and is also referred to as a "bottom." A good team of two or three mules or horses can pull a double-bottom turn plow, for instance, which is the same as two single-action plows on the same setup, throwing the dirt in the same direction. This type of turn plow, however, is different from a "double edged" or "double-action," turn plow. A double-action turn plow is a single moldboard that throws dirt both ways and can also be used as a middle buster. If we had owned one of those I would seldom have used our regular light-duty one-sweep middle buster. The only problem employing a double-edged turn plow would be horsepower, for a double-action turn plow is very heavy. A plow being heavy, plus having to be pulled through the ground, would be too much for one horse or mule. I would have needed at least a two-horse team, especially to bust, or throw in one pass, that big middle between the potato rows. With a double-edged turn plow I would have had to make only one pass between each potato row. Now that would have been great and so pretty when I looked back at the row. Well, we didn't have a double-action turn plow or two good mules, so we did the next best thing—we did all that work with less. Busting a middle with a single-edged turn plow is a tough job. If you are not adept or skillful enough to bust that middle 100 percent with two passes, one up and one back, with a single-edged turn plow you still will not be done. You either keep making passes with the turn plow or unhook the turn plow and hook up to the middle buster and plow out the middle to finish the job quicker.

Here is how you avoid so much extra work when using a single-edged turn plow. The first pass should not be difficult at all. Using a right-action turn plow, peel off the entire right half of the dirt row, or middle. What I did the first pass was peel off ever so slightly more than 50 percent of the middle, but not enough to make a big difference in proportion. I did that because it is the second half that might give you trouble. In other words, turning ever so slightly more than 50 percent of the first pass allows you to hold the point—the leading or cutting part of the moldboard—directly under what should be a well-cut, vertical left edge of what is remaining of the middle, or dirt row, after you have made the first pass. Also, if you took off slightly more than 50 percent of the dirt row at first, you would now notice that the top of the remaining dirt to be turned is sloping to the right, which is the direction you are now throwing the dirt. This sloping effect will aid the plow in breaking the dirt loose and throwing it in place, right where you want it, at the same time leaving the plow with a much reduced propensity to slide, or scoot, to the left, out from under the dirt you are turning. Furthermore, if you had removed less than 50 percent during the first pass, as you were turned around and looking at the top left of the remaining dirt to be thrown, you would notice that it would be sloping slightly left, which is what you don't want.

The following are important reasons why I took off slightly more than half of the dirt row the first time. Taking off less could put more work on the horse and you in several ways. First, you would be trying to throw a deeper cut, resulting in turning more dirt. Second, the sloping left dirt would tend to fall left, down into the middle, and you don't want that.

Third, you are now farther away from the right edge of the dirt row, and thus unable to move the soil close enough around the plants. Fourth, your plow would tend to slide or scoot left, because you would be too deep, struggling, and have forced yourself to concentrate on too many things. Fifth, when the plow slid left it would be out of position, out of the ground, and you would be trying to get it back in. Sixth, now you would not be plowing anything, and the horse would still be moving forward, and faster, because he would now feel no resistance and would be thinking more and more that he was done. I could go on about what you would have done wrong, but I will say that if you hadn't panicked by now and started plowing up potato plants, you could stop the horse, back up, and insert the plow where you left off, or you could walk that horse—or "deadhead" as it is called—all the way around the patch and come back to where you left off.

Deadheading is having the horse pull the plow from one place to another while not plowing dirt, and the term generally refers to non-productive movement or work. Deadheading occurs when one presses down on the handles of the plow as the horse walks, to ensure that the point of the moldboard does not enter the ground.

So, you can do all that, or you can decide to rise to the occasion and "work it right" from the start. Besides, once you take a horse out of a patch, or work area, he'll think he is done and will walk your legs off trying to get away from that plow and you. Once a horse thinks he is done you will need more than a sugar cube to get him to return to that work area right then. Anyway, you now know what that big middle row of dirt was for: It all has to be around the growing plants. When you get it right or plow it properly, the potato plants will appear to be atop perfect rows.

Harvesting sweet potatoes in those days was hard

work, but it was fun and a rewarding time for me. I loved opening up the ground and exposing big, beautiful, fully ripened,
colorful sweet potatoes. Before you get to that point, though,
there are a few things you must do. Sweet potatoes have a long
growing season, much like cotton. That is why they produce
best in warm climates. Five to six months from planting to
harvest would be about right, as long as they are planted from
slips, young pre-sprouted plants, as opposed to cubed potato
eyes like Irish potatoes are planted. At harvest time, we would
chop the sweet potato vines off the tops of the rows and drag
them out of the patch. Now the potato patch would be clean
of vines and all the rows ready to be turned open. Once the
ground was turned open, the potatoes could easily be seen
and would be picked up. This is where the two-horse or two-
mule team with a double-edged or double-action turn plow
would excel. This plow will bust a perfectly deep middle and
lay those potato rows right open, one pass per row. The main
down side to busting a large row of potatoes with one double-
action plow is that some of the potatoes may be damaged or
even covered up with dirt again. You would just have to make
sure that whatever plow is used for this purpose is pulled along
well underneath the potatoes so they would not be damaged
by the plow. Since we had only one horse and one single-action
turn plow, we peeled off the two sides of the row first and
picked up those potatoes. These potatoes are easily picked up
at this point so they don't get covered with dirt by subsequent
passes. Then we would hook up to the middle buster, install a
medium sweep on it, and then lay open, or bust, the middle or
remainder of the potato row, thereby exposing the potatoes remaining in the row. When this process is followed until the entire patch is harvested, the ground of the patch is now already
turned for the winter—in perfect rows. So, the next spring we
would first fertilize the middles and repeat the plowing process

by applying the above-mentioned procedure of peeling off the big dirt rows to the middles, thus making the ground ready for planting slips again. Momma never bothered with canning any sweet potatoes, because when we harvested them we found some way to eat them about every day until they were gone. They were a favorite food that could be prepared several different ways.

Momma canned plums, pears, apples, and peaches, and just like all the other canned food, they would be gone before winter was over. Momma had a nice way of spicing up canned fruit. When she canned plums she removed the seeds and hulls (skins), spiced up the remainder, and called it "plum butter." My brother and I loved making "smothermies" from Momma's canned fruit. "Smother me" is a name we two gave to our hot-fruit sandwiches. We would cook a large thin flapjack in a skillet. We took the cooked flapjack from the skillet and put it on a plate or piece of paper. While the flapjack was still hot we poured a generous amount of Momma's canned fruit on half of it and folded the other half over the fruit, thereby smothering it. My favorite canned fruit for making "smothermies" was Momma's plum butter. She made it from a special plum that grew on trees around our house. They ripened red or yellow. They were unlike prunes or other big plums. I only saw them grow in the South. In those days, old abandoned homesteads still produced plums years after the people, and the house, were gone.

Somebody was always peddling fruits and vegetables. Momma would buy fruits, such as cantaloupes, watermelons, pears, apples, and peaches, from Mr. Tidwell. He lived in an area just outside of Plain Dealing and tended what people called "truck patches" and drove through the communities and the countryside selling the produce on old well-maintained stake bed trucks. As a little fellow, I remember him driving an old truck from the late 1920s, peddling fruits and vegetables on it. I just admired the technology of that truck, for its efficiency and simplicity. Mr. Tidwell grew the same things we did, but in much larger quantities. I can remember Momma buying from Mr. Tidwell quite often, for years. A woman named Cleo Jackson was another peddler, mainly of dairy products. Everybody called her Miss Cleo. She peddled her dairy items in a dark green mid-1950s Chevy pickup truck. Miss Cleo sported a big wide smile and always chewed a big wad of gum and could pop it at will, making it sound so good. She was very active and industrious, but sold us very little milk and butter because Sis Pearlie beat her to the draw by giving us free butter milk and butter.

In Bolinger in the wintertime—if that's what you want to call it in Louisiana—the worst we normally experienced was freezing rain. Measurable snow came every three or four years. A common sound after a freezing rain was the snapping or breaking of pine trees, as though the process was methodically and chronologically planned. It seemed as though every tree waited its turn to see which could pop the loudest upon breaking from the weight of the ice. I can remember standing outside the house many times just listening to see the direction from which the next "pow!" would come. When the trees and branches snapped, they sounded like high-powered firearms being discharged. I considered it a wonder of nature and would walk through the woods, enjoying an enhanced scent of pine and assessing the damage. This was how we acquired our fire wood. We would cut trees that were damaged or dead, but still standing.

Whenever the snow came, we considered it a treat and a blessing. Every so many years there would be an accumulation of two to four inches, at which everyone simply marveled. I can remember watching it come down as we looked out the windows. We were excited and talked about it as it fell. But most of all, we were cheering for a measurable amount so we could grab some bowls and run outside and pack them with snow. That is how we had so much fun making ice cream. We brought the bowls of snow back inside the house and hurried to add sweet milk and sugar, stirring it to a smooth thick consistency. What a good treat that was. It seemed as though winter lasted just one month—January. Usually the Christmas holiday was cold, but with little or no snow. Spring weather usually came quickly in February. In late February, the flowers would be growing and everyone would be in short sleeves.

At home in Bolinger, we raised hogs and chickens. We raised chickens more years than we did hogs. I think it was because the hogs ended up eating more than we did and required special high-maintenance care sometimes. And it seemed as though Daddy's attitude was that animals were to be eaten or worked, but not necessarily cared for. Whatever the case, though, Daddy definitely knew the procedure for butchering a hog. The whole family took part in butchering and preparing the hogs for winter food. We had a meat grinder, also called a sausage grinder, and a big salt syringe. Daddy would build a huge wooden box and use it for the "sugar curing" process. This is the only time I ever knew salt to be referred to as sugar. A special salt brine was injected with a big syringe into large cuts of meat such as hams. The salt removed all moisture from the meat, thereby drying or curing it for storage. Many times when the curing process is completed, the meat is then put through the "smoking" process. For this purpose, many people built a little out-building called a "smoke house." During the butchering process, we would very thoroughly clean the intestines. Intestines would be either cooked and eaten, or stuffed with ground meat. Cooked hog intestines were known as "chittlins" in the rural South. Ground meat mixed with chopped, dried red peppers and other select spices would be stuffed into thoroughly cleaned intestines and smoked to produce smoked sausages. Meat would also be made into sausage patties, without being packed into intestines. The sausage patties would be fried for immediate consumption or wrapped in special paper and frozen in storage for later consumption. I loved eating sausage patties.

One of my favorite events during hog slaughtering season was when Momma made crackling bread. Crackling was assorted bits and pieces of hog skin and other parts left over after the animal fat, or lard, had been extracted. We extracted the fat in the big iron wash pot that was in our back yard. We would cut up, or cube, the portions of the hog that were mainly fat and skin. We built a fire around the pot then poured

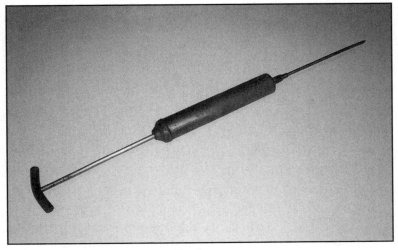

Syringe

This syringe was owned and used by the Arthur Ford family of Bossier Parish, Louisiana. It was used to inject a special salt into various cuts of hog meat, a process called sugar-curing. Sugar-curing rids the meats of all liquids and moisture. This syringe is two feet long, with a 6 inch perforated needle. (Courtesy of the Arthur Ford family.)

the cut-up meat into the heated pot. We stirred it frequently until the hot grease and fried skins were separated. We then dipped all the skins, or cracklings, from the pot, leaving the hot grease. The grease was then dipped out and poured into empty lard buckets, to be used for cooking. The cracklings would be cooked with corn bread or enjoyed alone as a tasty snack. A big chunk of that crackling bread mixed in a big bowl of simmered peas or beans, with a few cooked pieces of okra scattered on top, made a heavenly mess.

Chickens, a source of food that we raised at home, were manageable because we raised our own corn and could also buy a sack of cracked corn now and then for feeding purposes. We had quite a few chickens at one time and a chicken house, commonly called a henhouse, surrounded by a chicken-wire fence. Attached to the rear of the henhouse, near the top, was a structure of little cubicles where the hens would lay eggs. The hens accessed the structure by a board leaning to it from the ground. The leaning board had little strips of wood nailed across it at intervals, allowing the hens to climb the board. We kept two or three roosters around, and they were quite competitive. We called baby chickens biddies, and they were the most precious little things. I was more worried about them than anything else when I realized they were growing up to be our food, or someone else's food. I remember how people prided themselves on raising "pullets." They were called that mainly because of the youthful tenderness of their meat. When Momma got ready to cook chicken she would have one of us catch the chicken, and she would wring its head off. I hated the chicken-killing process. The last straw for me was when Momma made me catch a chicken and either wring its neck or chop its head off. Well, Momma didn't take no for an answer, and I knew it was either that chicken, or me. I remember disliking it when I saw people wringing the necks of chickens. Then

I found out why people would just wring the chicken's neck. I had one hell of a time trying to get that chicken to quit moving on that chopping block. For some reason Momma never asked me to do that again. I guess she had to teach me that chicken and dumplings didn't just pop up on the table. As our priorities changed, we eventually quit raising chickens and hogs.

There was a section along Highway 3 in Bolinger that spanned about an eighth to maybe a quarter of a mile, from C.G. Rich's grocery store on the south end to the Israel Light Baptist Church on the north, on a hill where the highway curved slightly left to a little downgrade. Just a little farther north was Highway 537, which I felt marked the very end of the strip to the north. At the junction of Highway 537 and Highway 3, on the south corner, was C.A. Rodgers' store. But the main part of this particular strip on Highway 3 was where Bolinger Road, off which we lived, intersected Highway 3. Just for the record, Bolinger Road is now called Bolinger Cutoff Road. This strip was referred to by Bolinger Negroes as "The Front." C.G. Rich's store commanded the most frontage on the southeast corner of Bolinger Road and Highway 3. On the northeast corner of Bolinger Road and Highway 3 once stood a Henry Rodgers store, and next to it, on the north side, stood the Dew Drop Inn, a little juke joint. Once upon a time, the Dew Drop Inn was a jumping joint. The Henry Rodgers' store eventually closed, and the building remained empty for a spell. A few steps behind these buildings, along Bolinger Road, was another little building that someone tried to make into a store. It was short-lived. Then that building eventually became Shipps' Grocery, run by Clifford Shipps. I remember Clifford was a polite fellow and acted like a real "good ole boy." Just east of Shipps' Grocery, next to its dirt parking lot, was a quiet little dirt road that ran north, from Bolinger Road, along the edge of a pine forest. A row of houses stood along this ungraveled dirt road on the west side of it, across from the forest. Right on the corner of this quiet little dirt road and Bolinger Road on the east side of Shipps' dirt parking lot stood two big oak trees. These two big trees stood about seven feet apart. There was a wide heavy-duty plank, or board, that spanned the distance between the two trees. The board was nailed onto wooden support blocks which themselves were nailed to the trees. This setup was known as the "roost pole." Just about any given time there would be two, three, or more old Negro men sitting on the roost pole, gossiping.

Uncle Lara Layton, my mother's uncle, would often stop at our house for me to fix something on his bicycle. He would let Daddy and us know that he was headed "over on the Front." Uncle Lara was a short and very dark-skinned, cigar-chomping man with a strong constitution. He walked slightly bent over from the waist and his whole body shook with every step he took, and he was bow-legged. He always wore a huge, expensive black cowboy hat, dressed in black, and around his neck he sported a colorful bandanna, usually with a red background. He spoke in a baritone voice and did strum the guitar a bit. Uncle Lara traveled by bicycle. As long as I can remember, he had a really fancy red bicycle with chrome-plated fenders. He had reflectors facing front and back, and two baskets, one attached to the front of the handlebars, supported by a bracket attached to the front wheel sprocket, and the other one attached to the rear of the seat, supported by a bracket attached to the rear wheel sprocket. The baskets were thereby "suspended" over the front and back fenders. On top of the handlebars on both sides he had warning devices, a horn on one side and a bell on the other. Coming from the ends of the black rubber hand grips that covered the ends of the handlebars were pretty little, thin, colorful plastic strips, about five or six on each side, which waved in the wind, especially when the bicycle was moving. Everybody knew when Uncle Lara came down the road because he tooted his horn and rang his bell. Daddy said Uncle Lara looked like a tumble bug riding a bicycle. Once when Uncle Lara stopped at the house to visit, we were sitting on the front porch, taking turns at the old acoustic guitar. Uncle Lara was playing that same tune he always played, which I learned to play just from hearing him play it. Daddy then got up from his rocking chair and walked into the house. He went to the refrigerator, removed the board that was propping the door shut, and bent over to look inside. I didn't know what he was looking for, because I knew it was empty. I guess all of us had a habit of doing that, hoping that something good would somehow appear. Daddy then straightened up and opened the little freezer hatch. He reached in the freezer and retrieved a box of Melorine, which was the only thing in there. Melorine was a fluffed-up substitute for ice cream. You had to eat it while it was fluffed and frozen because if it melted it ended up as nothing. The folks in the South called ice cream "cream." Daddy yelled out, "Ring!" That is what Daddy called Uncle Lara. Uncle Lara had his head down, going at that guitar. Daddy yelled out to him again, "Ring!" Uncle Lara suddenly stopped playing, looked and leaned to his left, near the opening of the front door, and yelled, "Yeah!" Daddy said to him, "You want some cream?" Uncle Lara yelled back to him, "Is it cold?" We laughed at that one for years.

Things were quite active over on the Front. Next to the Rich's store, they had a cute little cement-block building painted white, with glass windows on the front and halfway down the sides. There were two little service windows in front. Shading the front of the building over the service windows was a fancy little port supported by little metal posts anchored in a concrete hardstand. Both port and hardstand spanned the width of the building. This was a nice little drive-up fast-food service

they called the "Dairyette." In the 1950s and 1960s Charles
Gray Rich and his wife Dorothy always demonstrated a real
talent for running a business. I just admired them. They always
had something pleasant to say to me, and Mrs. Rich simply
wore the most infectious smile. In those days they would frequently host activities that drew the public, especially Negroes.
For instance, they had a television set on a high stand between
the store and the Dairyette. Most of the men folk in the area
would gather there and watch the Gillette Cavalcade of Sports,
featuring the "Friday Night Fights." I remember winning a bag
of groceries for our household in a drawing there one night. I
felt so happy and worthy because Momma and Daddy always
got groceries from C.G. Rich's store on credit. This was in the
late 1950s. In 2005, I took a trip back home to Louisiana. I
located Mrs. C.G. Rich and asked her if my folks owed them
any money. She said she had thrown all the papers away showing who owed them money, but that Momma and Daddy did
not owe them anything. She told me that when Momma and
Daddy bought food on credit, Daddy always came back later
and paid for it. I thanked her for letting me know. I remember when I was about ten years of age I walked over on the
Front to the store one day. On my arm I had glued a piece of
paper that had "shadow panel" written on it in big bold letters.
I remember thinking how cool that label looked, so I licked
the back of it where the glue was and pressed it on my arm.
Man, I thought I was so cool with that thing sticking on my
arm. When I walked into Mr. Rich's store, he asked me what I
had on my arm. I gave him some kind of a diplomatic answer,
because I had no idea what Shadow Panel was and never did
find out at that time. Mr. Rich then hollered back to Mrs. Rich,
who was at the meat counter, and said, "You know, he'd make
a good lawyer!" All she did was give the most beautiful smile
of approval. For years, I wondered if Mr. and Mrs. Rich were

after my heart or my money. Well, I didn't have any money so it had to be my heart, and they got it. The fact that this man would say something like that about a little Negro boy in those days spoke loudly to me about his independence and courage when the status quo staunchly required otherwise. Mr. Rich had a little garage-like building on the southeast corner of Bolinger Road and Highway 3. He always kept the two swinging doors in the front of the building shut and locked with a chain looped through some holes in them. Anyone could see inside the building by peeping through a small opening left by the swinging doors. There was talk going around about a brand new car in there. As soon as I heard about it, I walked over to the Front and peeped in and saw a big pretty black car. It was a new 1958 Chevrolet, the first model with the double headlights. The 1958 model was a complete change in design, which I think helped make the 1957 model eventually become such a beautiful classic. I remember thinking how pretty that new car looked inside that building and wondering who owned it.

When I was about ten years old I had another close call, almost to glory, at the hands of my sister a year or so older than myself. Up to this point, I had never heard her admit it, but she always had a temper to be reckoned with. She directed her anger at me one day and chased me much farther than I cared to run. I was alone in the back yard playing with an empty Pet milk can. It was the little nine-cent one. I was throwing the can in the air, letting it drop back to me and catching it. My sister came out of the house and walked over to where I was, telling me that she was going to take the can. I remember deciding not to say anything to her because of her quick, hot temper. I continued to throw the can in the air. When the can fell back down to me, she reached for it in a swiping motion. She missed the can, while I was still trying to catch it. In the confusion, I somehow knocked the can back into the air with my other hand. We both stepped toward it, reaching for it, and both missed. As a result the can fell and hit her on the foot. She immediately got really angry, saying how she was going to get me. When she said that, I immediately broke and ran, while at the same time she reached for me and missed. I continued to run, and she set out after me in hot pursuit. I dashed for the lane that went from our house to Bolinger Road. She surprised me with her no-quit stamina, so I figured I could shake her at the old wire gate that connected the fence surrounding our property. The gate set atop a small bridge that covered a little gully running across the dirt lane. I knew the condition of the wire gate because it was always breaking from opening and closing, and Daddy was always "volunteering" me to help him fix it. Well, running from my sister and not being able to shake her, I went for the weakest part of the gate, figuring I wouldn't break stride much, which would buy me some time to pull away from her. It worked—getting through the gate that is. So when I went through the wire gate and turned right, going past the first of two church toilets on the way toward Sis Pearlie's house, I slowed down to look behind me. I almost came to a complete stop, because I just knew my sister wouldn't be able to get through that gate easily because of the barbed wire, for it was bound to catch on her clothes, shredding them up because of her desperate movement, and send her galloping back to the house in defeat. I was wrong. There she was, almost touching me. I hit stride again. At the moment, all I could think of was getting inside Sis Pearlie's yard and running around in there, hoping my sister would stop the craziness. I didn't make it. Just about the time I started thinking that idea, I felt a thump on the back of my head and heard a pop. I immediately turned around and ran right past my sister to get back to the house, instinctively feeling something drastic had happened. I didn't feel any pain but felt something warm

on the back of my neck. I was still running back up the lane
when, to my left, I heard some noise. It was Miss Honey, running from the back porch of Sis Pearlie's house, having let the
screen door slam. Miss Honey was yelling, "Stop him! Stop
him!" By this time I knew I was bleeding badly, because I could
feel the blood soaking the back of my shirt and going down in
the back of my pants. I was still running. I heard Miss Honey
scream with a desperate voice, "Stop him, y'all stop him!" At
that time I looked over at her and she was gathering up her
dress between her legs to get over the fence that divided Sis
Pearlie's property and ours, on the west side of our sweet potato patch. I was still running, focusing my eyes and attention
toward our house again. I heard Miss Honey yell, "Go get the
coal oil!" I wondered what she was going to do with that coal
oil so I rounded the wood pile, turning right, and still running,
headed toward W.C. Root's house. I just got passed the wood
pile when someone grabbed me. I could feel Miss Honey holding me still and pouring coal oil on my head. I thought my head
was going to fill up with coal oil so I made an attempt to break
loose. Miss Honey tightened her grasp and told me to be still.
I held still and realized that she was trying to get the bleeding
to stop. She miraculously stopped the bleeding. She removed
my blood-soaked clothes and washed my head, face, neck and
back. I remember feeling alright after Miss Honey did that. I
later found out that my sister had picked up an old, rusty rasp
file and made a throw that Crazy Horse would have been proud
of. At that time I remember looking at my bloody clothes after
they were removed and being amazed. Fate had it that Miss
Honey was to visit Sis Pearlie for at least one special reason
that day. Only the passing of the years has put in perspective
for me the enormous deed of Alberta Haskin (Miss Honey),
who has long since passed on to Glory. Every time I think of
what happened, I silently thank that wonderful lady for saving

my life. My sister was in her fifties when she called me on the
telephone one day and apologized for what she did. I was all
too eager to tell her that I had long ago forgiven her, because
I considered it one of the unfortunate activities of childhood,
a part of growing up.

When all the poultices and other home remedies and
time itself didn't work to cure wounds and sicknesses there
was one thing besides castor oil that cured Southern Negroes
every time, so they believed, especially the old folks, and that
was something they called "asfidity." Spell it how you may, but
when it was about to be sprung on you, you either ran away
or you got better instantaneously. That was the stinkiest stuff
I ever smelt. Momma used to make it like no problem. Come
to find out, asfidity was an old slave cure-all concoction passed
down through the generations as a remedy. When Momma
didn't feel well, for instance, she would pinch a small amount
off and place it between her cheek and gum, and the rest of
us would clear out. The point I'm trying to make here is that
not just during slavery, but even when I grew up in the South,
seeing a doctor was quite the exception for most Negroes, not
the rule. With Southern Negroes, getting well was mind-over-
matter, establishing and maintaining something to believe in.
It helped you survive, because necessary financial and other
pertinent resources just weren't there.

Through the years, after we had moved back to
Bolinger and having worked some years as sharecroppers on
the Lake Bottoms, we were then trucked back to the Lake Bottoms to work the cotton fields. When we traveled on Highway 537 from Bolinger going to the Lake Bottoms, we would
pass a section of land that supported a few residents and was
known to the people as the "Nigger Ridge," sometimes also
called "The Ridge." I don't know who named it but that is what
people called it, no questions asked. And if someone lived over

there and was asked where they lived, they would say, "Over on the Nigger Ridge," or "Over on the Ridge." And no one would act surprised because the Nigger Ridge was the Nigger Ridge, just like Bolinger was Bolinger. There were several residents there, the most notable of whom were the Martins, Toy and Ida. Miss Ida, as we called her, was a regular on the cotton-chopping circuit and kept people, especially the young folks, laughing at her antics and sayings. She was always chewing her husband out about something. She and Mr. Toy were once riding in their truck near the Lake Bottoms, on a road in the wooded area just east of it, and Mr. Toy accidentally ran off the road into the woods, bouncing and hitting trees. After the truck ran over bushes and bumped some trees and then came to a stop, Miss Ida asked him, "Wheya gwine now?" Another well known resident of the Nigger Ridge was a man named Harry Brown. Harry Brown lived back in the woods a bit and mainly kept to himself. People called him other names, which I thought were undeserved and more disrespectful than fitting, like "hobo" and "hermit." I always wondered who the man was that consistently managed a big wide grin as he would just politely say, "Hi." My sister, Maude, would get the biggest thrill when I mimicked "Ole Man Harry Brown" during our little minstrel shows that my siblings and I held at home. Maude was very talented and taught us a lot of stuff about acting out personalities and showing off. In those days, the folks called it "showin' out." Maude would scrape soot from inside the stove or heater pipes, mix it with lard, spread it on her face, and do comedy and have us laughing. She would put on some of Daddy's old clothes, get in black-face, come to the front door and scare the heck out of the rest of us, acting like Ole Man Harry Brown. Highway 537 ran on past the Nigger Ridge on its way to the Lake Bottoms. Not far past the Nigger Ridge on 537 was a big hill. In those days from atop that hill you could see a wide panoramic view of the Lake Bottoms, and as far as one could see it looked like a hazy, dried-up ocean bottom. At the bottom of the hill, on the north side of Highway 537, was a huge pecan orchard. The owner of the orchard lived next to it and also owned cows and horses. Once past that, you were officially in the Lake Bottoms.

One of my favorite Bolinger people was someone whom I considered a great horseman, named Ben Root. All the Negro people knew him as Mr. Fan. If a horse were to be seen climbing a ladder I'd bet you Mr. Fan taught him. That man could teach a horse to walk on the moon. Mr. Fan worked for a rancher named Cartwright. It was Mr. Fan who let my brother and me ride his horses. He is the one who took in O'Buddy, our plow horse, and cared for him until the horse died. Thank God our horse died in the best of care, I always felt. During one of my early trips back home, I asked Daddy where O'Buddy was. He told me, "Fan got'em." I immediately made short order of a trip to Mr. Fan's house, and quickly asked him where Buddy was. Mr. Fan pointed the horse out to me. O'Buddy was out in a huge pasture with numerous other horses, which instantly met with my approval. He was quite a distance away but I could tell he was fine and happy. While standing there watching him I couldn't help thinking about how happy he acted the time I pulled a nail from his foot; he had been limping for days. I didn't bother calling to him because it only would have interrupted his grazing, and, maybe I was afraid he wouldn't have come anyway. One thing I knew for sure is that he was in great hands with Mr. Fan. I never saw O'Buddy again. My, how happy I would be to see that horse, and Mr. Fan, just one more time.

CHAPTER SEVEN
High School Independence

In the late 1950s Momma started seeking work outside the home. She found work at night in a café in Plain Dealing, along Highway 3, a couple of doors south of the Gleason Ford dealership. At that time Gleason Ford stood at the junction of Highway 2 and Highway 3. Highway 2, from that point, went eastward through the middle of downtown Plain Dealing and on to Sarepta and points beyond. Just about an eighth of a mile north of Highway 2 east, on Highway 3, Highway 2 extended west from Plain Dealing, through St. Mary and across the Red River to Hosston and Vivian, and on to the Louisiana-Texas state line. In Plain Dealing in the early 1960s, a business loop was constructed eastward, starting at Highway 3, connecting to Highway 2 west. It was a nice four-lane thoroughfare that by-passed downtown Plain Dealing, although only a block north of downtown and the existing Highway 2, then curved slightly and again connected up with Highway 2 east of Plain Dealing. After that project was completed that entire connector became Highway 2. The busy junction next to Gleason Ford consequently was no longer Highway 2. Momma worked nights at that café near Gleason Ford. The café was off limits to Negro patrons in those days. Momma and Miss Honey worked there at the same time for a while.

Momma eventually left that café and got a day job at the café of a utensil-slinging, red-faced white woman named Lucille. Miss Lucille's place was called the Louisiana Café, located in downtown Plain Dealing. What amazed me is that the woman could also talk politely. That woman made my Momma cry many times. She paid Momma three dollars a day and deducted eight cents from that, on the spot, for what she called social security. Momma showed me two dollars and ninety-two cents pay one day, after having worked over ten hours. Minimum wage hadn't reached Negro wage earners in those days. Momma worked for Miss Lucille for a few years and managed to reach some common ground with her. Momma said Miss Lucille cried desperately when she stopped working there.

By the time Momma established a working reputation in the cafés, she had already started a trend toward independence. She had embarked upon the road of marital separation. She started leaving home for extended periods of time and would then return. She started taking us little ones and showing up at the steps of Grommau's house. I remember it was during those years that my sisters Hazel and Maude relocated to a place near Pocatello, Idaho, with Poppa John and whomever he was living with at the time. We little ones were left to fight with Grommau, and Momma even left Grommau's house and lived in Texas for a while. Despite all this, and more, Daddy never left home. In late 1960 or early 1961, Momma left home for good. I was in seventh grade at that time. That was when Miss Helen Charles asked me how my siblings and I remained such beautiful, well-mannered children in the midst of such family confusion. I remember not knowing how to gather the words to answer her because I was shocked and ashamed that she even knew about our family situation. At that time, I didn't know how to tell her that I appreciated her complement; I didn't know how to tell her that I knew Momma and Daddy loved us, and I thanked my lucky stars that we had already been a family; I didn't know how to tell her that I had already learned that I must keep pressing forward, because in this life, "marking time" is moving backward. One lesson I learned at a very young age is that no one can predict where life is going to take anyone, and no one will ever walk in anybody else's shoes.

When breaking up was inevitable between Momma and Daddy, Daddy became an even more frustrated man. When Momma left home for good, Daddy started keeping food, like a loaf of bread and other food stuffs, in his trunk, where he kept all his personal things, such as old pictures of his family. This trunk was off-limits to us children and none of us ever bothered it. Daddy even kept the trunk locked. In fact, when we were home during Daddy's funeral in 1985, some of us stayed at the house in Bolinger, and I never once thought to check inside that trunk, and to this day don't know what happened to it. I do know that a relative somehow ended up with Daddy's pictures from that trunk. Good times at home when Daddy opened his trunk and showed us pictures of Grampa and Gramma Ford were absolutely special treats, and my siblings and I knew that Daddy wouldn't have given those pictures up to anybody, not for all the gold in the world. I borrowed the original pictures from this relative to duplicate them, and then returned them to her, because she had somehow acquired them from my father.

During Momma and Daddy's breakup, she and the kids lived for a long while in Plain Dealing with Grommau Mamie Layton. We continued to go to school and work the cotton fields. I always maintained close contact with Daddy and our Bolinger home. At times I would walk the railroad tracks from Plain Dealing to Bolinger and from Bolinger to Plain Dealing. In the summer of 1962, my brother and I with our cotton-chopping money helped Momma buy a house that set empty on Plain Dealing Lake Road. It was in a grassy field just west of some fields of sugarcane grown by a hard-working Negro man who made his own syrup. He owned his own mules, mill, and all. Momma had the house moved to Plain Dealing, slightly southwest of the downtown area. My brother and I cleaned it up, did some work to it, and moved in. Momma never did move into the house. She immediately moved to California, where some of my sisters had already settled. My brother soon started hurting for support and direction, so he moved back in with Daddy in Bolinger. Well, I wanted to leave all that responsibility too, but somebody had to look after that house. I made some payments for Momma to some white man who lived in a section of town where all white folks lived, and where I didn't care to go. In fact, it was the old Crawford Hill. Needless to say, there I was fifteen and sixteen years old living all by myself. My hand had definitely been forced, but I hung in there. Quitting school was not an option with me because I had already decided that nothing was getting between me and my high school education. I was determined to earn my diploma because I had come too far the hard way to turn back.

In September 1962, I went to downtown Plain Dealing looking for a job. The 1962-63 school year had started; I was in tenth grade and had finished up another summer chopping cotton, but still needed money for living expenses. I had decided to just go from door to door of the downtown businesses looking for work. I started at a store a few doors north of the drug store, across the street from the seed and grain store that stood next to the railroad tracks. I walked in and told the man I was looking for a job and asked if he had any work. The man acted polite and talked favorably. This was on a Monday and he told me to come back Thursday, that he would have something. I was so happy that I decided to spend some of my cotton-chopping money on a pair of sweetnin' waters. In those days Southern Negro people called dress pants "sweetnin' waters." If you had on dress pants, people would stare and wonder what you were up to. Some people would even ask you, "Where you git them sweetnin' waters?" Anyway, I was so happy about what the man had said to me that I didn't even bother checking anywhere else that day for a job. I had even spent the next few days excitedly thinking about how I was going to spend my earnings. Thursday rolled around, and I had taken a bath in the old number 3 tub and even put some Vaseline on my hair, trying to slick it down and look good. I don't remember what shirt I wore or where I got it. I walked into the store smiling and told the man I came back for the job. When the man gazed at me and wasn't smiling I knew I had something coming— I was in uncharted waters, indeed. First he yelled, asking me "What job?" I said, "You told me to come back Thurs…" I hadn't finished saying the word Thursday when the man interrupted me and yelled, "Boy you git otta heya, I ain got no job fer you!" I was so shocked I turned around immediately and walked out the door, happy to have something left of me. This man had just yelled at me like I was a stray dog. I may not have been a stray dog, but damn if I didn't leave there with my tail tucked. Well, with the mind I had, you know I wasn't going to give up.

When I was walking away from the rude acting white man's store it seemed like my mind began to clear up. It had been clogged up with thoughts of justice, freedom, peace, nice people. Then I decided, "to hell with that." The man angered me and did push me to the murky waters of bad thought, but I wasn't about to be stupid and jump off the deep end, for people like him don't even realize that their actions will come back to haunt them somewhere down the road of life. I had suddenly begun to realize why Negroes had their own businesses, honky-tonks, and churches, for instance. Segregation and bad treatment will help do that, you see. The clearer my mind got the faster I walked, toward the "Low End." I walked right on down to Macon McCauley's store and found a job. Besides, I wasn't going to buy new sweetnin' waters for nothing. I started talking to Mr. Macon and don't even remember filling out an application or signing anything. In fact, in those days filling out job applications wasn't customary in Negro culture, because employment was simply not meant to be gainful, under segregation and Jim Crow. Mr. Macon hired me right then, and the rest was history. I was hired to do everything in the store. I pumped gasoline, swept the floors, worked the cash register, kept the shelves stocked and neat, etc. Now, the first store I went to was a white man's store, and I got insulted. The second store I went to was a Negro's store, and I found work. I had to face segregation and Jim Crow head on and make it somehow work for me. First, it got me and the rude white man out of each other's face. Second, it caused me to once again have the determination and the will to keep going and find a job. Mr. Macon, as everybody called him, was a very polite and methodical mulatto business man. He also had some acreage and grew cotton. His brother, Ephraim, whom everybody simply called Ethan, owned a store in St. Mary. Mr. Macon's store in Plain Dealing was located in the heart of an area known as the Low End. I don't think I have to tell you what side of town this was. It was the Low End that took me to another level of creativity. It helped show me the way to deal with, and get along with, many different types of people.

Inside the back part of the building that housed Mr. Macon's store was a nice little restaurant that I didn't know was there until I started working in the store. I liked the chili served there because it was thick and loaded with meat and beans. There was a building called "T & L" in an area behind Mr. Macon's store, where many teenagers and young adults hung out. Mr. Macon's store occupied a corner lot with frontage on two streets. Next to the store, to the north, was a barber shop. Across the street from Mr. Macon's store and the barber shop, on the west side, was the part of the Low End that caught my attention the most. It was what I always thought of as the stables, because it reminded me of stalls where horses are housed. It was a series of connected juke joints that lined the street as one long building. The roof was low and appeared to be almost flat. There was no wasted space and with the joints side by side, you could walk out of one, turn, and walk right into another. This is where I could hear the great rhythms of pure unadulterated Blues and the original forms of Rock and Roll, straight from the masters. Bobby "Blue" Bland, B.B. "Blues Boy" King, Little Richard, Antoine "Fats" Domino, and Chuck Berry, just to name a few, were "rockin' the joints" in the Negro South many years before their popularity reached "mainstream" America. These and many other great musical artists, like James Brown, Johnny Taylor, Wilson Picket, and Otis Redding, were already musical giants in segregated Negro America. All these and many other great musical talents influenced me. In those days, it sounded like those artists were singing to, and for, the people in the cotton fields. Many of their songs still remind me of the cotton fields of the South where many of us spent so many years of our lives laboring, wishing, hoping, and thinking. When I was in high school I loved tuning in to radio station KOKA to listen to B.B. the "Bird Brain," an awesomely talented DJ who kept everybody in high spirits and jumping with "Check In" in the morning before school. I also tuned in to radio station KEEL to see what Leslie Gore, Rick Nelson, Elvis Presley and some others were up to. Daddy liked listening to radio station KWKH which featured lots of news and also played great Country artists like Hank Williams and shows like the Louisiana Hayrides. I liked singing and playing Country and Western songs, for they were just as touching as the Blues. The guitar players that turned my head were Charlie Christian and Wes Montgomery, for they had styles like many of us Southern boys had. The guitar artistry of Les Paul was simply wonderful to see and hear. Chet Atkins was really at home with his melodic, syncopated Country guitar. I think just about all of us got our starts in church. Sam Cook and Lou Rawls were well-traveled Gospel singers in those days. The Soul Stirrers and the Mighty Clouds of Joy were on the cutting edge of the great Gospel quartets, quintets, and sextets back in those days. When I was in tenth grade, and a while in eleventh grade, I played guitar for a Gospel quintet called the Hearts of Harmony. That was when I lived by myself in the house in Plain Dealing. We played many churches in and around the Bossier Parish area. Many times while we rocked the country churches, white men would come right up to the windows, and watch. It would often be two Caucasian heads sticking completely inside the windows and I never saw, or heard of, anyone turning them away. In fact, I saw people move over so the men could see better. When I had left the South I found out that I wasn't the only Negro musician plagued with accusations of playing the Devil's music, and many of the same people danced to it and simply enjoyed listening to it. Daddy later told me that as soon as I left home, two white men from a television station in Shreveport came to the house looking for me. I never knew who they were. There was a building along Highway 3 and Crabapple St., on the northeast corner, on Plain Dealing's south side, from which the music and voices of young people could be heard blasting at night, especially on the weekends. It was a segregated roller skating rink for the white kids only, on the Negro side of town. In 2005 the old building still stood, but was for sale.

At Carrie Martin High School, no reference was made to a middle school or even junior high. There, sixth, seventh, and eighth grades were referred to mostly as secondary school. The sixth grade was in a controversial position, however. There were always debates and arguments about whether it should be part of elementary or secondary. Many people just called it upper elementary. I don't remember anything being resolved about it, and I considered the issue one of the down sides of a twelve-grade school system. The sixth grade never disappeared, and the beat went on.

I was recruited into the high school band as a drummer when I was in fifth grade because by the time I reached fourth grade I was already playing a snare drum with a big, authoritative ego. In those days we wore used uniforms that were not tailored and, early on, were not even in the school's colors. There wasn't a helmet to fit me, they all were too big, and the legs of the trousers were too long. I rolled up the pant legs on the inside and pinned them. I tightened the helmet's chin strap all the way to the last hole, but it was still too loose. When we marched on the football field and in parades I had to march tilting my head back, peeping from under the bill of the helmet because it would always slip down over my eyes. I lived with the inadequacies because I loved playing. I had excellent rhythm, quick wrists and hands, great reflexes, could read music, and had an ego to match them all. I played rings around the high school drummers because of it. Many times when we marched in parades, other drummers would get tired, get long looks on their faces, and just lay out, resting, because they knew I would continue playing, no matter what, along with the bass drummer and the cymbal player. Every time they laid out like that, I kept the band marching in time by simply making up cadences as we marched. I will never forget the time we marched in a Shreveport parade. The parade stopped, and everybody was just standing around waiting. I could sense that no one was happy with the delay. I noticed some really pretty majorettes in the band behind us. They were moving around in an anxious manner. I asked the bass drummer and the cymbal player to join me in some cadences. We three stood facing each other, playing. It was easy for me, because I knew all I had to do was play a creative, well-maintained syncopated 4/4 beat, and improvise away. Before long we were in the middle of a crowd of musicians watching the action; those majorettes surrounded us three players, dancing like there was no tomorrow.

I managed to stay in the band about six years, until the end of my sophomore year. When I returned to school for my junior year, after having spent another summer chopping cotton, I found that my economic situation had changed dramatically, and I needed to make some big changes, some milestone decisions, once again. I was supporting myself and had to rise to the occasion. I had to leave behind all the fun things in school if I were to survive in school. I did some figuring. I thought that if the Carrie Martin High School principal and all the teachers had college degrees in order to have their jobs, I would need one too, even though my sight were not necessarily set on becoming a teacher at that time. Therefore, I always held my education in high regard and disciplined myself accordingly. So I had to let go of my first true love, playing music the way I could, but I always felt I would get back to it.

I talked to Mr. A.J. Brewer, the janitor of the elementary school buildings, about a job. I was immediately hired by the Bossier Parish School Board through Mr. Brewer. Right after I was hired as a part-time janitor, Miss Boyd, the cafeteria supervisor, came to me and asked me to work for her in the cafeteria. I remember that was a job everybody was trying to get because free lunch was a perk. I didn't ask Miss Boyd for the job, because I felt that my place just wasn't inside that cafeteria. But there I was, actually turning the job down. Miss Boyd must have had a lot of respect for me because she also approached me just a few days after that and asked me to talk to her son about direction in life. She looked straight in my eyes and told me I had vision and direction. I remember being absolutely stunned, but flattered. This wonderful lady told me some things about myself that you just don't expect a junior in high school to hear. Of course, I declined to talk to her son. I thanked her for having such a flattering opinion of me, but I preferred letting her talk to her son. Miss Boyd's son was nearly my age, and I felt that if someone doesn't want to look in a certain direction you can't make them, no matter what you say. It's like what Louis Armstrong told a woman once when she asked him what jazz was. He told her if she didn't know, don't mess with it. Miss Boyd was a woman whom everyone respected highly, because she was a person of her word and complemented that integrity with courtesy. She reminded me of one of my seventh grade teachers, Pearle Gipson; she spoke softly, but carried a big stick. Miss Boyd so melted my heart with her kind words that day that I darn near apologized for those times I snuck in the lunch line. Her kindness worked wonders for me because I never snuck in the lunch line after that.

I told Miss Boyd I had already found a job working for Mr. Brewer. I remember her eyes stretching and her face smiling as she complimented me on getting the job with Mr. Brewer. She even told me that she was sorry I couldn't work for her. I admit, that lady made me feel like I was on top of the world, getting that kind of approval from such a well-respected grown-up. I asked her if my brother could have the job. She said yes. But somehow, our cousin ended up with the job, and he stayed on it for the duration of his high school years. Good for him.

Miss Boyd had put together a star-studded staff. Most of the women who worked in food service for Miss Boyd could have been supervisors or even restaurateurs. The one who most frequently comes to mind is Lillian Johnson. When Miss Lillian, as she was called by everyone, smiled at you, you knew you were doing something right because she expected you to be at your best at all times. They prepared food that was absolutely world class. They all wore hair nets, and they wore white uniforms like nurses. Their faces shined from cleanliness, as well as their hands. Every day they served meals that were complete and nutritionally well balanced. I haven't seen their procedure or style anywhere since. I remember two dishes that drew most of the Carrie Martin High School population to the cafeteria on the days whenever they were served. One was chili-beans over rice; the other was fish; the fish lunch was served every Friday. The plates we ate from were of hard, durable, plastic and had divided sections. The plates, silverware, glasses and cups were constantly being washed and sterilized and never did I see old food particles stuck on any of them. Dessert was served with every meal and my favorite dessert was peanut butter squares with raisins in them.

I worked as a janitor my junior and senior years. My work time was immediately after school ended every day. I earned thirty-three dollars a month, paid once a month. This was a tremendous help to me as I worked my way through high school. In the summer, I chopped cotton and also helped Mr. Brewer some, mowing grass, washing walls and ceilings and doing some building repairs. I also helped my Uncle Van Wade with his cows and helped him clean the graveyard where Daddy and his relatives are now buried, as is Uncle Van. And Uncle Van actually paid me for helping him clean what was at that time called the Ford graveyard. In those days even the cemeteries in the South were segregated.

When we chopped cotton and caught the cotton trucks in Plain Dealing, one of the locations was the corner where Mr. Honess's (Earnest Burnham) snow cone shop was. When we got dropped off at the same place, Mr. Honess always came out and fired up that snow cone machine and drew a crowd. Mike Jones and Boy Charles were two men who were noted for making their living by hauling people to and from the cotton fields. Most of the school kids spent their summers working the cotton fields. When I came along, we didn't have Boy Scouts and summer camps. Practically none of the Negro parents had gainful employment that would make life pleasant, simply because of the oppressive tenets of Jim Crow and racial segregation. Jim Crow determined everything, from the cotton fields to the mayor's office to the governor's office. Plain Dealing politics did not include Negroes in those days, so we relied heavily on the barber shops, churches, radio and some television, school, etc., for social and political information, and on the cotton fields, rivers, and timber for economic survival. Strategies of segregationists are complex and dynamic, for altering the course of nature is quite an undertaking.

My tenth and eleventh grade years were very, very busy for me. Also, the summer between ninth and tenth grades was busy, in addition to working the cotton fields. I remember getting left behind on the Lake Bottoms by the cotton truck one day. I don't remember who was driving the truck, but being left was a frightening situation. After making the day in the cotton field we stopped at the C.A. Rodgers store in Wardview, where they told their Negro patrons not to crowd the store. They allowed only a few inside the store at a time while all the others stood outside and waited. Everyone politely honored the request. I was in the last group that day and ended up suffering the consequences because of the actions of a lead-footed, impatient cotton truck driver. I walked out of the store just in time to see the truck pulling away. Needless to say, hollering, "Wait, wait, wait a minute," didn't help me. I immediately assessed my situation and made a conscious decision not to panic. Thinking and surviving this situation was mandatory. I realized that walking just wasn't going to cut it, but at least I had two ways to go in case someone would give me a ride. It was a long way to Plain Dealing both ways, via Bolinger, Highway 537 east, and a long way to Plain Dealing via St. Mary, Highway 537 south. I decided to do something I hadn't done before, just go ahead and ask someone for a ride because I was tired from working the cotton field all day and just didn't feel like walking such a long distance. Very soon a man pulled up in a pickup truck. He got out and went into the store. I stood just outside the door, waiting for him to come out. As soon as he came out I greeted him politely and asked him was he going to Plain Dealing. He said yeah, and I asked if I could get a ride with him, and he said, "Yeah, git in." I excitedly walked to the passenger side of the truck, and the man walked to the driver's side. He quickly got inside the truck. I opened the door to get inside. Then he yelled, as he gestured with his head and right hand with thumb, "Git back there, can't you see her here!?" Fact is, I was so excited about getting a ride I didn't notice the little girl or dwell on the fact that they were white folks and I was Negro, which, by the way, is what the man was getting at. It is quite interesting how minds work. I quickly reacted to what the man said and jumped in the back of the truck. The man took off toward St. Mary on Highway 537 south and that is when I started thinking. I thought deeply about why he would yell like that in the first place. When the man yelled I focused on the little girl and then shut the door. It was the expression on the kid's face that bothered me, and it also told me a story. I was sensitive to her feelings, not his or mine. What was she getting from this? What would the child's future hold because of this? I felt, how blind and stupid some of us are, causing us all to lose. I couldn't help realizing how a person can see something in someone else that is not even there, and how they can insult one's intelligence through misinterpretation. I remembered actually wondering to myself, "How long will it take for people to wake up?" I reflected on the situation during the entire trip, periodically noticing the little girl looking at me through the window. The man stopped in front of the new bank that was built in Plain Dealing, across the alley from Miss Lucille's café. I climbed out of the truck and thanked the man. I started walking away when he said something to me in a polite tone of voice. The fellow even had almost a slight smile on his face as he asked, "Do you know George Ashley?" I was quite surprised, pleasantly, I must say, at his change in character. I said, "That's my brother." He said, "I know him." I then asked the man, "What is your name?" He said, "Pittman." He then drove off. I then thought about how I was told long before by Momma and Grommau that my half-brother, George, "Buddy," as we all called him, was a playmate of the Pittman boys. That was when we lived on the Lake Bottoms, sharecropping, on the Perry Pittman plantation. Of course, I learned long before my tenth grade in school that you might want to be kind to people because you never know who you might see again down the road. Historically, the Perry Pitman property was acquired from the twelve hundred acres of "Ford-inherited" property.

In high school, in the South under segregation, Negro boys in the ninth through twelfth grades were the New Farmers of America, NFA. The white boys were the Future Farmers of America, FFA. Our agriculture teacher was named Edison George Hogan. We called him "Prof," not sounding the "f." I remember having a little talk with Prof about the two organizations. I asked him why there were two different names. I had been thinking that "New Farmers" simply meant high schoolers, just getting started, and maybe "Future Farmers" might have been the college boys, more advanced, on the way to becoming farmers, no matter what race of people they were. Man was I wrong, with that kind of thinking. Well, obviously it bugged me enough to ask Mr. Hogan, and that is when I learned the difference. I thought having two different organizations was senseless, for farming is farming. I felt that if you know how to farm, you know how to farm, no matter who you are. I took it personally, as a slap in the face, to be labeled "new." I told Mr. Hogan we weren't new. I remember asking him who decided that, and why do Negroes get referred to in inferior ways. He looked at me, right in my eyes without saying anything for a few seconds, and then said, "That's the way it is." Now to my way of thinking, under that system the white boys would be the future in farming, moving on, and the Negro boys would always be new, without a future in farming, moving nowhere. That bothered me like the Civil War bothered Abraham Lincoln and the Vietnam War bothered Lyndon Johnson. To my mind, that was totally unacceptable. The reality I knew about Negroes farming certainly wasn't new. Based on what Mr. Hogan told me, I felt, "That may be the way it is, but that is not the way it will stay." I quit beating Mr. Hogan"s ear off and went on my way.

Prof had a big fat hog named Jelly Roll. Jelly Roll died from heat exhaustion one day, right after we had marched in downtown Plain Dealing in the Dogwood Parade. Mr. Hogan was a tall, neat, heavy set Negro man who was the favorite of all the high school boys. He was a smart man, socially adept, and always had us laughing about something. Now and then somebody would push Prof the wrong way, and we all would have to get paddled with that big board he had. There were three holes in it and a handle cut to fit his hand. That damn thing hurt! I will never forget the time when Prof had one of his paddle sessions, after which he talked to us while we were still snuffling and sniffling and some of us still dropping some pretty big crocodile tears. He told us how, "At the beginning of the school year all the textbooks on that table but one had covers." He then said, "Now all the textbooks on the table don't have covers, but one." We all laughed like crazy about what he said. That was how Prof always redeemed himself, and it worked every time. He was right about the books. Prof ran the concession stand, a one-room setup located in the north end of the agriculture building itself, where everybody went to buy candy, bubble gum, and all their other favorite snacks. The agriculture building was of wood construction, housing just the classroom and the concession stand. A solid wall separated the two rooms, with no access door between them. The classroom was long and rectangular, with one door for the entrance and exit. The west wall had a long blackboard along it, and the east wall had big windows along its entire span. Sometimes Prof would still be in the concession stand a few minutes after recess and lunch breaks were over, and the students would have already gathered for class. When the students got loud and rowdy Prof would hit really hard on the wall. Most times it worked, quieting the students down. Sometimes it didn't work, and that's when Prof would come to the classroom steaming. He would then retrieve that three-hole paddle board and have at it. Once, Prof had one of his mad days and told us we were a bunch of FBIs. We started looking at each other, smiling and wondering why he was complimenting us on being smart FBI people. Somebody spoke up and asked him why we were FBIs. He said, "Because, y'all just Fat, Black, and Ignorant!" Everybody, except Prof, laughed like crazy, and then class proceeded. And I remember very vividly us guys calling each other FBIs until I graduated from high school.

It wasn't Prof's wall banging, or his paddle board that increased my heart rate though—it was what happened at those big windows that lined the east wall of the building. This was where the high school boys mastered their craft of girl-watching, and I was no exception. When I was in elementary school I remember noticing how those "old-looking" high school boys looked out those windows. Well, it eventually became my turn, and I thought about that when I looked out the windows, but for some reason never thought of myself as an old-looking high school boy.

It was in my junior year, the spring of 1964, a beautiful spring day, and I was looking out a window of the agriculture classroom. Everyone was excited about spring, and being outside, and wearing less clothing. And it was less clothing that caught my eyes, as two girls walked past, heading toward the concession stand and talking to each other. The windows and floor of the agriculture building were relatively high off the ground and the view was down, onto the passersby. The two girls walked past me as though they didn't see me. The girl on the right caught my attention with her mannerisms and the way she walked. She had on a dress that ended around the top half of her knees, just fine. Her legs were pretty, and she walked with pride and authority. I never took my eyes off her. Just before she and her companion reached the corner of the building, about to go around the corner, this pretty girl suddenly looked back at me, directly in my face, and flashed the most radiant smile. I noticed her face blushing excitedly. She made my day like no one else had.

She turned out to be my first and only high school sweetheart. I don't even remember how we started talking, but we wrote each other letters and dated some. My first date with her was in my Uncle Van Wade's new Ford truck, the first one Ford made to look and drive like a car. It had the shifter on the steering column and was one pretty truck. During the summer months she worked in the home of cattle rancher Abe Martin, with Mr. Martin's wife. While there, she would write me some nice letters that I enjoyed reading. I liked reading about her trips to Beaumont, Texas, to visit relatives. She would sometimes shop and very excitedly show me what she had bought. I loved seeing her smile. She was truly my one and only love in high school.

Dosie and Me – 1964
(Courtesy of the Arthur Ford family.)

CHAPTER EIGHT
Back Home In Bollinger

By the end of my junior year I was pretty fed up with having to look after the house in Plain Dealing and being so busy. I didn't mind being busy, but I did mind going crazy trying to stay focused. So, I decided it was time to make another landmark decision. I had reached a real crossroads. Do I hold on to a falling star, by trying to look after Momma's house that even she wasn't living in it, or do I let go and survive? I figured after the chaotic ups and downs I had experienced in the last couple of years in Plain Dealing, home in Bolinger would be a pleasure. That quiet back porch and the sights and sounds of the forest of tall pine trees were weighing heavily on my mind, and it took no time to make my decision. I moved back home in Bolinger. I made a conscious effort to make that last summer and school year my best, at home. That's exactly what I did, and I let no business interfere with my pleasure. I saw my Daddy bursting with pride and happiness, for his two "bulls," as he always called my brother and I, were home to stay. I did my last summer of plowing with a mule Daddy had bought. Daddy and my younger brother and I did lots of things. That time was another special one, bonding with home.

In 1964 when the Louisiana State University was still segregated, I wrote a letter to the admissions department requesting a curriculum catalogue and other information concerning admissions, including an application for admission. This was not an attempt to rile anybody up down there, it's that I actually thought I could be a civil engineer, and I found out that LSU offered a degree in that, and I thought nothing about the university actually being racially segregated. Well, how was I to know that I was going to need all that math, and it was a good thing that I didn't show my face at their door. Also, without giving it a second thought, I always believed in the concept of "opportunity" that our "democratic" way of life promoted, and was just being spontaneous about how I felt. I received the requested materials from LSU and held on to them until Daddy informed me one day, when I was home on leave from the Vietnam War, that my sister Hazel had burned them up, along with some other important books that I had ordered and received from the Berry School of Horsemanship in Pleasant Hill, Ohio. Daddy told me that Hazel said my books were the work of the Devil and had to be destroyed.

Near the end of my senior year I was awarded a one

Daddy and his "Bulls," Summer, 1964
Left to right, Daddy holding his grandson Michael, my brother Perkins, and me, Arthur, Jr. (Courtesy of the Arthur Ford family.)

hundred dollar academic scholarship certificate to Grambling College. I was pleasantly surprised by the award, but I never claimed it, for life's decisions already had me headed outbound. That was the time when a classmate of mine named Stanley came up to me and stood directly in front of me with the strangest look on his face, gazing in my eyes and said, "Fode, you can do anything cainchy?" I don't remember what I said back to him but I did consider it sort of a back-handed compliment, about which I was never angry.

On graduation night, some special things happened to me. Miss Harris (Miss Lee), the teacher who came to the second grade classroom and took me back to first grade after I had already passed first grade, came up to me in the hallway and handed me the only graduation gift I received. She just smiled, and I accepted it and thanked her. She said nothing and just turned around and walked away, and I never saw her again. The greatest compliments I received on graduation night were from two of my classmates, my peers, for if your peers give you special regard you have undoubtedly made an impact. I was standing just outside the main entrance of the high school building near a car, talking to someone after we had walked. The two fellows, at different times, told me the same thing. They both said they wished they had my abilities to do what I did all through school. I was just speechless, for they were my peers, from whom came the most critical comments throughout my school career. The only thing I could do was look at them and thank them. I know that night the fellows were speaking from their hearts, probably because, as I later learned, they had flunked. Perhaps they had come out to see their classmates step up and claim the coveted prize, something they missed, for they had undoubtedly realized a little too late what was important, as well as the frightening fear and feeling of being left behind.

Under Jim Crow and racial segregation in the South, powerful Caucasian segregationists caused and enforced a lack of any opportunities for Negro people to advance themselves in any manner. Under that separate and unequal system we were deliberately and unconstitutionally denied, in many ways, whenever and wherever possible, access to the economic resources and liberties that would have led to the pursuit of happiness. Under the system of racial segregation a Negro, especially a man, young or old, was considered uppity if he demonstrated any desire to move forward in life and show respect for himself, and he was highly likely to be harassed, especially upon becoming a young adult. I experienced a very frightening and dangerous incident in the spring of 1965, a month or so before I graduated from high school. On this particular day, just before school was out for the day, I had asked my good friend Ardis Lee Heard to go over some math problems with me. Heard was always smart in math and demonstrated it by doing well on exams and in class participation and homework. He proved to me that he was an intelligent person by the way I saw him do things. Other than one of my great math teachers, A. Morris Lee, I had never asked anyone for help in any subject matter before. I guess Mr. Lee saw I was bound and determined not to flunk, so he told me I needed to: "stop thoughtin' and start thinkin'." I immediately started thinking. So I asked Heard if he and I could do some studying together to prepare for an upcoming math exam. He said yes, and I told him I would drive over to his house after I got home from school and work. He agreed, and that is what we did. I was feeling really good about our study session afterwards and was on my way home when I was stopped on Bolinger Road, just after turning off Highway 3, slightly east of Clifford Shipps' Grocery store and the Roost Pole, on a section of the road guarded by woods on both sides. The officer was deputy Reese

Hardcastle. He went quickly passed me and then got right in front of me and pressed on his brakes. We both stopped. I had never been stopped by a police officer before. We both got out of our vehicles. I leaned on the front-left fender of our truck, on my right elbow. The deputy wasted no time coming up to me, right in my face. He opened up yelling, "Boy, what you mean whistling at them white girls!?" I said, "I didn't whistle at any girls; I don't know what you mean." At that very instant a

Arthur Ford, Jr. – Summer 1964

This night my brother and I sang Curtis Mayfield's "People Get Ready" by The Impressions. I loved playing Mayfield's beautiful guitar melodies. (Courtesy of the Arthur Ford family.)

pickup truck pulled up beside me and three white men got out and stood just to my left, next to me, watching me. I knew right then I had to use my head. I made a quick decision to be really quiet and still. I was one shocked and angry fellow, but I stuck to my decision. The deputy then came even closer to me, almost touching, but I stood my ground with my eyes fixed right on his face. I had already noticed some weapons on a rack, mounted in the back window of the man's pickup truck when he pulled up. The deputy quickly tilted his head to his right and yelled out, "Oh yes you do boy, you know you ain't supposed to be whistling at no white girls!" I was still looking right in the deputy's face. That man had one red, sunburned face. The deputy yelled out some more stuff about white girls. I deliberately stayed focused on his face, hardly batting my eyes. I admit that took some doing, and I was becoming rapidly impatient but managed to remain still and quiet. Suddenly, without warning or hesitation, the deputy stopped yelling in my face, turned around quickly, and briskly walked to his car, got inside, and drove away, leaving the three men there, standing still and gazing at me. Then the three men got back into the pickup truck and drove away. Immediately after all the men left I remember just quietly standing there for a short time, still leaning on the truck, thinking about what had just happened. I then climbed back into our old black and white 1949 Ford three-quarter ton pickup truck, with those huge tires that they put on them back in those days, a truck that I was so proud that we had, and drove home.

When I arrived home I told Daddy what had just happened. Daddy then told me that Reese had stopped by the house before he came looking for me. Daddy said he had told Reese that he would go with him. He said Reese told him no. And Daddy said he told Reese that there will be no hitting and he said Reese told him there wouldn't be. I remember taking a moment, when Daddy told me that, to be so proud of him because there he was standing up for me when he didn't have a leg to stand on against that deputy, anymore than I did. And needless to say, I was still puzzled as to what was going on. I knew that I was entitled by any standard to know what that traumatic situation was about, but needed a little time to think of how I would investigate and get to the bottom of it. In the meantime, I went into the house and got my drumsticks and pad and walked somewhere not far from the house and practiced some technique. After a while, I went back to the house and walked up the front steps, and there the deputy was, sitting on the porch talking to Daddy and patting his feet, acting jolly. I remember wondering to myself, "How can this man be over there smiling and acting happy when I damned near just got killed?" As I walked up the steps, the deputy leaned forward and asked me, "Whatchy got there, boy?" I politely said, "Drum pad," and kept walking into the house. When the deputy left the house I asked Daddy why the deputy had come back to the house. Daddy said Reese came back to apologize, that nobody had whistled at the white girls. Daddy said Reese said it was the Cartwright girls who had lied. I remember feeling so relieved because the whole question I wanted to ask was answered, right there. I thought about how I didn't know much about the Cartwrights but had always respected them because they appeared to be so productive. But how it all came about was still puzzling to me. So I decided to backtrack, to retrace the afternoon's events, from the time Daddy drove to Plain Dealing to Carrie Martin High School to pick me up from work, and after.

When I got off work, Daddy was already parked in front of the school waiting for me to come out. He was sitting inside the truck on the passenger side, evidently expecting me to drive. I told Daddy that Perkins, my brother, was still at the school and wanted a ride. It wasn't long before Perkins and Milton West, who had just then asked for a ride, climbed into the back of the truck. So I was driving, Daddy was riding inside the cab on the passenger side, and the boys were riding in the bed of the truck. I then worked my way over to Highway 3 and headed north to Bolinger. As we approached Bolinger I remember having glanced at some movement, to my left, that had caught my peripheral vision. It was two girls riding horses in a pasture. People rode horses, so it meant nothing to me, and I harbored no more thoughts about it. I continued driving home, where I dropped off Daddy and the boys, and then I went over to Heard's house. Only when I retraced the events did I understand what happened. There I was, eighteen years old, a young man, a young Negro man—who, by the way, had never whistled at any woman or girl. That has never been my style. Just as I saw the girls riding horses, the girls saw our truck go by, with boys aboard. The girls evidently decided to have some "fun" causing trouble, using a serious situation, against which there is little or no defense for a man, which they knew would draw attention to themselves and to us, causing action, which evidently was what they wanted. So, they falsely accused a Negro boy of whistling at them, knowing that someone else would not see it as fun and would kill at the drop of a hat, without thinking, upon hearing that kind of talk. Out in the middle of an isolated area I got stopped and had to deal with a traumatic incident. I was unarmed and outnumbered by men with guns. Daddy was at home not knowing whether I was alive or dead. A big price was paid that day, all because of racist, and female paranoia. I can only thank my lucky stars that cooler heads prevailed in that situation. The men drove off, as they should have, and, in my mind, through the years, I always commended them for that. But what I cherish the most is that this powerful, Southern Caucasian law man apologized to my

Daddy. By all standards, I hold that in high regard. My brother and I talked about that incident years later, because I wanted to know his accounting of what happened, and if anyone on the back of the truck possibly whistled. He said nobody whistled. This meant, to me, that Deputy Reese Hardcastle really did a great human service, for situations like that cause wars, and he prevented a bloody war because he was intelligent enough to know that a man like me will defend his innocence, and because he knew a new day was dawning. The girls had lied, and Reese did an honorable thing by having them own up to it. And in those days a white man simply did not apologize to a Negro man, but Reese did.

Reese Hardcastle was the same law man who shielded me from an older woman in earlier years in similar circumstances. People called her Miss Shug and she called me "Bread" when I was a little fella, which I did not at all like, but I lived with it. But when the woman got old and accused me of hanging around her house, I had a problem with that and told Momma about it. Momma said she reported it to Reese Hardcastle. Momma said Reese told her that Miss Shug was suffering from hardening of the arteries. I quickly put that behind me and moved on and never had any more problems with that woman. I still think of deputy Reese Hardcastle as a guardian angel in those times, protecting an innocent Negro boy from dangers the boy simply didn't understand, or didn't even know were there. If Reese were alive today I would make a special trip home to thank and commend him for a job well done. Sadly, Daddy told me years later that Reese Hardcastle was found dead in the woods. I would also commend the Cartwright people for realizing, and recognizing the truth, and not jumping the gun. That took intelligence, and I tip my hat to them.

It was in the forest, in the summer of 1964, where I

again faced death, only to defy it again. One day Frisky, our dog, came home with a greatly diminished midsection, with a flat, empty-looking nipple area, hanging way down. I knew she had given birth to her puppies somewhere. Nature had blessed Frisky with puppies several times before and I knew she would only leave her babies in desperation. I immediately set out to find her litter. I took to the woods behind the house, figuring from experience and instinct that she probably went that way. I also knew that it wouldn't be sight that would find the puppies; it would be sound. I walked slowly and quietly, listening for the sounds of puppies. It wasn't far into the woods behind the house, about one hundred yards, where I heard and found the puppies. I went straight to them. There were several of the pretty little things. They were another litter of Frisky's trademark babies. They were all predominantly white with brown and black spots. And once again it was Miss Kizzie Root's dog that had been the winning suitor. In all of Frisky's litters there was at least one just like him, with that big intimidating black patch surrounding one eye. The puppies were underneath a bushy forest undergrowth where brown leaves had accumulated. I dropped to my knees in order to get a better look at them, get a count, and then start to rescue them. I then bent forward and reached as far as I could under the bush to get the most frantic one. Suddenly, at the end of my outstretched arm, right at my fingertips, the head of a snake drew back, impulsively, probably from the quick advance of my hand. I hadn't seen the snake because of its camouflage against the leaves. When the snake quickly drew its head back is when I saw it, and I jerked my hand back to my body with spontaneous quickness, at the same time noticing the snake's entire body, coiled in a perfect striking position. It appeared to be a snake that had the design and colors of a timber rattler, and its heat sensor, or tongue, was in action. I don't know why the snake didn't strike at my

Arthur L. Ford, Jr.
High School Graduation, May 29, 1965
(Courtesy of the Arthur Ford family.)

hand. Needless to say, getting off my knees from under that bush just might have been quicker than lightning, because the next thing I knew I was back in the front yard of the house, never having counted or rescued the puppies. Frisky somehow got the puppies home herself.

As awesome as the days and times of our survival on the Lake Bottoms were, they only served as a springboard to Bolinger and Plain Dealing society. Wardview is now mostly cow pastures and hay fields. There are locked gates connecting well-built fences with "No Trespassing" signs posted on them, where before there was constant human activity which seemed as though it would never end. And except for the Littles and the Gores, hardly anyone lives on the Lake Bottoms any more. In my mind Wardview can't possibly be forgotten, for it was the bridge that brought us over.

To me Plain Dealing itself was like home, too. Not just because the surrounding settlements were considered and referred to as Plain Dealing, but because there is where I lived, attended school, played, and socialized. The town of Plain Dealing was the hub" of plentiful human activity in north-central Bossier Parish.

Home is where the heart is, and for me it is Bolinger, Louisiana. That is where Momma and Daddy solidified the family and experienced the most trying times. Gramma and Grampa Ford lived and prospered in Red Land, Bolinger, and Plain Dealing. They died and are buried there.

It was the cotton fields, school, and the good old folks back home that shaped me. But most of all, it was the majestic and dynamic presence of the woods, the forests of towering pine trees among which I played, developed, and grew up to be a young man, where I played and sang my music for free, and where my siblings and I belted out loud, harmonious tunes that echoed supremely through the backwoods at night.

It was in the woods from whence came the most beautiful sounds and sights, including those of a boy and girl who may have stolen away, where the sight of a moonlit night through the pine trees was romantically sublime. Wonderful sounds of the birds were like sweet music to my ears. And after the sounds of all other birds of daylight had silenced, there was one bird that took center stage to put on a touching, clock-work performance of closure. It sang the saddest refrain to a day's work at its twilight that I ever heard. It was the song of the Whippoorwill. And when the Whippoorwill sang, I cried.

EPILOGUE

In the principal text of this book I insisted on keeping the discussion true to the racially segregated years up to and including May of 1965 which was the month and year I left the South. When I left the Plain Dealing, Louisiana, area it was still totally racially segregated where I grew up. That is why I referred to those times as part of an Original American Experience; a direct connection to the institution of Slavery; something not scripted by the mighty Movie Moguls of Hollywood; something not created or produced by the Brash Barons of Broadway. However, it was something that touched the lives and impacted the destinies of people all over the world.

I was compelled to write this section at the insistence of a good friend who was quite adamant about the thought that people would want to know about my life past or beyond the Original American Experience. Just in case my friend is right in his thinking, I decided to give the readers at least a brief accounting of my life after having grown up in the Deep South.

The day after I graduated from high school in May 1965, I caught the first thing smoking, a Continental Trailways bus, headed west to Los Angeles, California. That was when you still could get picked up along a country road or highway. I remember the segregated waiting rooms in Shreveport, Louisiana, upon my departure. I arrived in Los Angeles with burning ambition and burning eyes. I had never heard of smog before. Everybody kept telling me I would adjust to it. I didn't. I was chasing an education, but was also determined to holler at my mother and some of my sisters who had already taken up residence there.

I was in California only three months, and was admitted to Los Angeles City College without a dime to my name. I witnessed the start of the 1965 Watts riot, standing upon a huge piece of excavating equipment, right on the northwest corner of 116th St, Imperial Highway, and Avalon. It was a horrible sight that just broke my heart because where I'm from I only knew of people trying to build. I liked the bright lights and the city activity, watching businesses operate, and people move about continuously. I loved visiting Griffith Park quite often during that time when just a dirt road wound up to it. There was a breathtaking view at that location overlooking Los Angeles, and the Observatory even in those days was majestic. The turning point for me in the big city occurred at the corner of 108th Street and Central Avenue immediately after I turned off Central onto 108th heading west, when a bullet pierced the windshield of the car I was driving and put a hole in the steering wheel instead of me.

I then moved on to Michigan and managed to survive two years at Western Michigan University before coming face to face with three years of active military service during the peak of the Vietnam War. I did two tours of duty overseas, one in the Middle East, near Istanbul, Turkey, just outside a little village called Chokmokli in 1968-69, and the other near Stuttgart, Germany, in 1970. I loved the Turkish people wherever I went. They were always very welcoming and helpful. Sometimes as duty driver I would make a scheduled stop in the early morning in Chokmokli. The kind and jovial people would eagerly serve me a very tasty hot drink that was red in color. They called it Chi, a kind of tea. The folks were so polite and humble.

One high point in my military career occurred when I spent my last six months in Germany on TDY as a Touring

Entertainer. My peers insisted on calling me "Funky Fingers Ford" on our "Hard Rockin' Soul" show. I laughed at the name until the MC started bringing me to the stage by it, drawing loud applause. After that successful tour I was asked to organize a band and go back on tour. I obliged them, and went on to become an award-winning bandleader, but declined their request to travel all over Europe after having completed the second tour of the Baden-Wuerttemberg District. During my leisure time I loved taking trips to downtown Stuttgart and buying those tasty Bratwursts with the tart spicy mustard. I enjoyed playing at the Atlantic Jazz Club one night with an

**Art "Funky Fingers" Ford
Mannheim, Germany, August 5, 1970**
The above photograph is one of a few that managed to remain in my possession. It was taken during a live performance in Mannheim, Germany in 1970 and handed to me later. In those days I laid the microphone right inside the piano. This allowed the amplified speakers to pickup the eloquent natural sound of the many grand pianos that I played. (Courtesy of the Arthur Ford family.)

Australian jazz band after hours. After my military service, I played some music in parts of Michigan, but my last public appearance was at the VA hospital in Battle Creek, Michigan in March 1983.

All my overseas performances were keyboard/vocals. Guitar and keyboard performances were in the States. I enjoyed the club dates I played at Fort Sheridan, north of Chicago, while stationed there the last six months of 1969. During that time I lived off base in Waukegan, Illinois, for a while.

The day after I got home from military service, I met the young lady who eventually became my wife. She and I raised six productive children, virtually all of whom acquired college degrees and are professionals in their respective industries.

I made my living in the transportation industry and eventually operated my own trucking business, Cargo Transfer, Inc., before I sold my equipment and subsequently opted to pursue other life-long interests.

My proudest achievement in trucking occurred when I honored a contract lasting more than a year, hauling precast, concrete beams and concrete oversized loads from Rochelle, Illinois, to Kalamazoo, Michigan, to the Detroit Metro Airport's "world's largest" parking ramp, getting every load delivered undamaged. Some other proud accomplishments along the road of life include:

Harness racing; licensed, United States Trotting Association, Trainer/Driver/Owner. I made it to the winner's circle a few times with horses that I trained and was happy to see my wife and kids have fun at the races. They also helped me with the horses at home and sometimes at the training track. I drove in Qualifiers and Fairs at that time. There is a trailer-load of rules, regulations, opportunities, and privileges that make the race tracks safe for horses, participants, and fans. Any horse can go fast running, but harness horses must possess the abil-

SHIAWAY LIBERATOR   Sports Creek 3-16-91 Purse $1200
Larry Lake Driver Art Ford Trainer Arthur & Beverly Ford Owners
Time To Spend 2nd   One Mile Pace Track Fast Cerramar 3rd
:29-2 1:01- 1:30-4 2:01-3 25.80 8.80 4.20 Photo by L.W.Wilson

"Winner's Circle"
Swartz Creek, Michigan – March 16, 1991

I was proud and excited to be involved in harness racing. It is a family sport. I loved being accompanied at the races by my wife and children. Frederick, standing down front smiling, is our oldest son, now an Aerospace engineer. (Courtesy of Sports Creek Race Course; L. W. Wilson, photographer.)

Natalie (top), Frederick (middle), and Douglas (bottom)

Fun times at the races. Above are photos of "Restricted Area" passes and "Groom" licenses for children accompanying their parents at the races. It was fun signing for the kid's passes, and watching them sign. The three youngest, Natalie, Frederick and Douglas often accompanied Dad and Mom and helped with the horses. At the races Douglas often teamed up for some serious play around the paddocks with his buddy Wesley. They kept me on my toes more than the watchful eyes of the racetrack judges. (Courtesy of the Michigan Office of the Racing Commissioner.)

ity to exhibit specific gaits or actions with their legs while going fast. So, if you want to delve into true equine talent, go to the harness races. And all the hard-working people who make it happen deserve unending applause.

Golf: I participated in a 1975 Michigan Public Links golf tournament; we had fun airing out our drivers from the tournament tees at the Indian Run Golf Course, a 7,600-yard layout back then. I hit some really good approach shots, too, but couldn't buy a putt that day. I did not make the cut, but was so very happy to be there and participate.

I am forever fascinated by true American and World history, especially the little known-historical facts that can be documented of the lives and activities of human beings. Look behind doors; you may be surprised to find something totally different than what you may have thought. Look at the back of a house sometimes instead of the front; you may be surprised to find what it is really all about. Look at a person's real track record in life, rather than the words someone may have whispered in your ear.

APPENDIX

Southern Rural Negro Dialect

The names of people, places and things were almost always pronounced differently by southern rural people, especially the Negroes, from their official or actual assigning. Slaves did not go to school to be educated so they learned everything they knew from listening to and watching others. They picked up patterns and ways of speech by listening to other slaves as well as their masters. For instance, an overseer would say wheelbarl, a slave would say wheelbar, or wheelabar simply because that is what he heard. As you can see, neither overseer nor slave was grammatically correct but they learned to understand each other through common communication. That's the South for you. Historically slaves have passed on their reluctancy to pronounce or add consonants like "r" and "l" or "s" to words and phrases. Even today many Black Americans display that same tradition. You must keep in mind that even though the times about which I write in this book were times of racial segregation and Jim Crow in the mid 1900s, or mid 20th century, they were themselves directly connected to and passed on from the times of slavery in the United States.

There were even different degrees of the Slave-Negro dialects. I will never forget a woman named Margie York who lived in Bolinger not far from where our family lived. Miss Margie, as she was called by the Negroes, maintained the Slave Dialect so strongly that even I had to sometimes ask other people what she was saying. I remember Miss Margie being so sensitive to the plight of Negroes that she would become very emotional and cry when she spoke.

Southern rural people seldom called or referred to one another by their real names. They would use nicknames of adjectives, or nouns, no question. The following are just some of the words and phrases that characterized Southern Rural Negro Dialect during racial segregation and plantation life when I was growing up in the South. Following each entry is a sentence exampling the usage of the selected words and phrases.

There are many more specifics and variations of the southern rural dialect than what I have listed. My intention is to convey to you the fundamental method of speaking the dialect and understanding it. You can even test yourself by combining words and phrases, making your own sentences. If I were to write a textbook for classroom purposes on this dialect I would include much more detail on particular rules that apply to make the student more aware and able to understand and speak it more fluently. Several "Rules" follows the dialect examples.

I think that if peoples of the world communicated more efficiently we would understand more about each other and how we are saying the same things, which indicate to me that we are more alike than different.

After studying the examples and rules provided, I believe you can create a few sentences of your own. Also, the more you study and understand the dialect you will learn how to condense dialect words, phrases and sentences to Standard English. You will also learn to insert correct English words where they were only implied in dialect expression. You can go a step further by seeking, conversing and communicating with some of the many people who still live and have direct connection with what I call the Southern Rural Negro Dialect.

DIALECT EXAMPLES

Dialect *Sentence*	Translation *Translation*
Ahm *Ahm goin home.*	I'm *I'm going home.*
Aiy " " " " *Aiy gau hit em.*	Is not Aint I'm not Aren't Are not *I'm not going to hit him.*
Aintchy *You gau hep me, aintchy?*	Aren't you? *You're going to help me, aren't you?*
Brang Cher *Brang cher, June.*	Bring it here *Bring it here, Junior.*
Cainchy, Caintchu *Caintchu go too?*	Can't you? *Can't you go too?*
Caiy *I caiy tote dis.*	Can't *I can't carry this.*
Caus *We ken go in caus day heya.*	Because *We can go inside because they're here.*
Cone, Roshenier *We picked cone deday.*	Corn *We picked corn today.*
Dare, Daya, Yonder, Nare *He went ova yonder.*	There *He went over there.*
Dat, Tat *Git offa dat!*	That *Get off that!*

De, Dah, Te
Ghea em da ball.

The
Give him the ball.

Dee, Day, Ay
"
Day all sade de same thang.

They
They're
They all said the same thing.

Deez
Deez ain't de ones.

These
These are not the ones.

Dis
Dis fi hot!

This
This fire is hot!

Em
Day git em?

Him
Did they get him?

Em, Uhm, Ehm, Dem
Day caught all uh ehm.

Them
They caught all of them.

En, An
Mae en Jack gau run.

And
Mary and Jack are going to run.

Feh, Fer
Good fer ye.

For
Good for you.

Fo
Quitat fo yah hurtcho sef.

Four, Before
Quit that before you hurt yourself.

Fode
Fode Mota Compny made dat.

Ford
Ford Motor Company made that.

Foid
Dat hoss kick Jame on de foid.

Forehead
*That horse kicked James
on the forehead.*

Foke
Alla de ole foke came.

Folk
All of the old folks came.

Fole
Fole alla deez cher close.

Fold
Fold all these clothes.

Frunt Rume
"

Front Room
Living Room

Alluhm in de front room.

All of them are in the living room.

Ghea
Ghea em alluhm.

Give
Give him all of them.

Git
Git te rope.

Get
Get the rope.

Gitchu
I ken gitchu anudda shoe.

Get you
I can get you another shoe.

Gau, Gwa, Gwy, Mau, My
Ahmau wauk down yonder.

Going to
I'm going to walk down there.

Gwine
Wheya gwine now?

Going
Where are you going now?

Heya, Cher
Heya day come.

Here
Here they come.

Hep
Hep me tote tis.

Help
Help me carry this.

Hotten
Issyu gau hotten nat comb?

To heat something
Are you going to heat that comb?

Ice petata
Dau plantat Ice Petata.

Irish Potato
Don't plant that Irish Potato.

Ignut
Dat boy ignut.

Ignorant
That boy is ignorant.

Iss
"
Iss foa clock.

Jess
Iss jess de sane thang.

Ken
Ken Joe do dis?

Lack
I lack it lack dat.

Less
"
*Less go down yonder
en play some ball.*

Limble, Supa
"
"
Dat boy sho supa.

Looka, Lookit
Looka dat car daya.

Lookin Glass
*Momma, Junior broke
tat lookin glass.*

Natcha Bone
"
"
Dat chya natcha bone ugly.

Nau
Nau, I caiy sey dat.

Its
It is
It is four O'clock.

Just
It's just the same thing.

Can
Can Joe do this?

Like
I like it like that.

Let's
Let us
*Let's go down there
and play ball.*

Flexible
Limber
Supple
That boy's body sure is supple.

Look at
Look at that car there.

Mirror
*Mom, Junior broke
that mirror.*

Naturally born
Sure is
Absolutely the way it is
That child sure is ugly.

No
No, I can't say that.

O, Ole
*Dat O man wauk beah
footed allde time.*

Old
*That old man walks
barefooted all the time.*

Offa
"
Gitcho feet offa dat dess.

Off
Off of
Get your feet off that desk.

Oughten it
Dat oughta fit, oughten it?

Shouldn't it?
That should fit, shouldn't it?

Outta
Git outta heya.

Out of
Get out of here.

Po
Po foke dau have no money.

Poor
Poor folks don't have any money.

Pure Dee
"
"
"
"
Dat boy is pure dee fat.

Absolutely
Real
Really
No doubt about it
"Very,very"
That boy is very, very fat.

Putty
*Puttysa speca pup
unda wagin wheel.*

Pretty
*Pretty as a speckled pup
under a wagon wheel.*

Rabbished
Dat boy rabbished dat gal.

Raped
That boy raped that girl.

Rat now
You gotta move dat rat now.

Right now
You've got to move that right now.

Sced
She sced te wauk cross tat.

Scared
She's scared to walk across that.

Sed, Sade   Said
Dat aiy what I sed.   *That is not what I said.*
Seed   Saw
"   Seen
Ah seedju over yonder.   *I saw you over there.*

Shiffero   Vanity
Momma, Junior hitcho Shiffero.   *Mom, Junior hit your Vanity.*

Sho' Nuff   Sure
"   surely
"   surely enough
Dis heya smoke meat sho nuff good.   *This smoked meat sure is good.*

Sitchy   Such a
Aiy know she do sitchy thang.   *I didn't know she would*
                                                       do such a thing.

Soma Dat   Some of that
Ken I haah soma dat?   *Can I have some of that?*

Soyshee   Sausage
Dis soyshee is sho nuff good.   *This sausage sure is good.*

Spose   Suppose
I spose so.   *I suppose so.*

Sposeda   Suppose to
Dat aiy how is sposeda be.   *That is not the way it is suppose to be.*

Spy Glasses   Binoculars
Deh sell spy glasses in nat sto.   *They sell binoculars in that store.*

Sto   Store
Dey got lotta dat in nat sto.   *They have lots of that in that store.*

Sunt   Sent
Daddy sunt dem de git wood.   *Dad sent them to get wood.*

Tote, Care
He caiy tote alla dat wood.
Uh, Uhv
He took all uh it.

Carry
He can't carry all that wood.
Of
He took all of it.

Waus
Looka dat big waus.

Wasp
Look at that big wasp.

Wauses
Dem wauses ah stang ye.

Wasps
Those wasps will sting you.

Wheelabar
Brang nat wheelabar.

Wheelbarrow
Bring that wheelbarrow.

Wid
Gwon wid dem.

With
Go on with them.

Wranch
Wranchout deez cher close.

Rinse
Rinse these clothes.

Wuhden
"
Dat boy wuhden eem ready.

Wasn't
Weren't
That boy wasn't even ready.

Yall
"
Yall come backte seeus.

You
You all
You all come back to see us.

Yaa, Yeah
Yaa, go headen do dat.

Yes
Yes, go ahead and do that.

Yistidy
I seedem yistidy.

Yesterday
I saw him yesterday.

Ye, Yah
Yeah, dey look good on ye.

You
Yes, they look good on you.

Yo
You need som on yo head.

Your
You need something on your head.

DIALECT RULES

Following is an example of rules that may seem quite contrary, however, they do apply.

RULE –   When multiple dialect substitutes are used they are applied according to the word that precedes them, even though they may be acceptable behind other words.

Example: We will take the dialect substitutes for the word "That" which are Dat and Nat. If the standard English sentence is "Do that right now" the dialect sentence would be "Do dat rat now" instead of "Do nat rat now." The correct dialect selection is "Dat" instead of "Nat." In other words the "D" sound would be more applicable in the sentence behind the word "Do" than the "N" sound. Notice that in the following sentence the dialect substitute "Nat" is more applicable behind the word "When." Dialect is "When nat boy wauk he wobble." English is "When that boy walks he wobbles." The substitute "Dat" would be incorrect.

RULE –   In many instances of dialect speech extra substitutes are used in a manner that might seem unnecessary but are usually applied for the purpose of emphasizing a point or conveying a message or thought.

Example: Dialect is "You comere rat now!"
            English is "Come here now!"

RULE –   The consonant or letter "s" is dropped from
            many words when speaking Southern Rural Negro
            Dialect.

Example: Using the same sentence we used previously dem-
            onstrates an applicable example. Dialect is "When
            nat boy wauk he wobble," without the letter "s."
            English is "When that boy walks he wobbles," with
            the correct application of the letter "s."

RULE -   In dialect when certain "undesirable" consonants
            are dropped from some words fewer syllables are
            pronounced.

Example: In the word "Every," with three syllables for in-
            stance, drop the consonant "r" and one syllable
            is eliminated leaving only two, resulting in dialect
            substitutes "Ehva or Ehvy." Therefore, in dialect it
            takes less effort to pronounce the word. For writ-
            ing purposes a rule would be to add "h" to achieve
            desired sound.

            Keep in mind that slaves had to be great improvis-
            ers and innovators, even without schooling some
            of them managed to write letters to loved ones,
            writing words the only way they knew how: The
            way the words sounded to them.

**Arthur Lee Ford, Jr. (left)
with Odie Lee "Sonny" Gore, Jr.**

ABOUT THE AUTHOR

Arthur Lee Ford, Jr. was born in 1947 at Shreveport, Louisiana. Although his family's home was located in Bolinger, Louisiana, Ford spent much of his youth working the cotton fields in the nearby sharecropping community of Wardview (also known as the Lake Bottoms). An inquisitive youth, Ford had an unquenchable thirst for knowledge and education. Aggravated by the social limitation of the segregated Deep South, Ford fled Louisiana for California the day after he graduated from Carrie Martin High School. Having witnessed firsthand the violence of the 1965 Watts Riots, Ford relocated to the more peaceful community of Kalamazoo, Michigan, where he studied at Western Michigan University. After serving several years in United States Army, Ford returned to Kalamazo, where he married his wife Beverly, with whom he raised six children, and launched several successful business ventures, including his own trucking company. Ford has a tremendous passion for harness racing, music, history, and in his younger days, golf. *When the Whippoorwill Sang* is the first of many books that Ford plans to write.

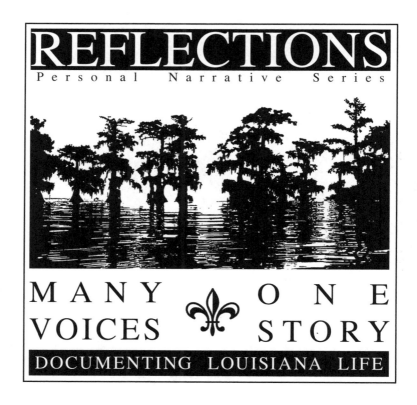

REFLECTIONS

Personal Narrative Series

MANY ✠ ONE
VOICES STORY

DOCUMENTING LOUISIANA LIFE

The Reflections Personal Narrative Series seeks to give a voice to the broad range of diverse individuals that populate Louisiana and in doing so to document the many lives that comprise the story of the Pelican State. From the Bossier Parish sharecropper to the New Orleans law school professor and everyone in between, these are the stories that define who we are.